THE GIFTS OF LAY MINISTRY

THE GIFTS OF LAY MINISTRY

BARBARA DENT

AVE MARIA PRESS
Notre Dame, Indiana 46556

© 1989 by Ave Maria Press, Notre Dame, Indiana 46556

International Standard Book Number: 0-87793-407-X

Library of Congress Catalog Card Number: 89-84285

Cover photography by Jim Whitmer and bottom left, Gene Plaisted.

Cover design: Elizabeth J. French

Printed and bound in the United States of America.

Contents

5

Note on abbreviations and terms used

Church: Dogmatic Constitution on the Church

Laity: Decree on the Apostolate of the Laity

Liturgy: Constitution on the Sacred Liturgy

Missions: Decree on the Church's Missionary Activity

Modern World: Pastoral Constitution on the Church
in the Modern World

Ecumenism: Decree on Ecumenism

diakonia: service

kenosis: self-emptying

kerygma: witness of the Word

koinonia: Christian fellowship of love

martyrion: witness, including that of blood

metanoia: conversion, change of heart

There is a variety of gifts but always the same Spirit; there are all sorts of service to be done, but always to the same Lord; working in all sorts of different ways in different people, it is the same God who is working in all of them.

—1 Corinthians 12:4-6

He continually distributes in His body, that is, in the Church, gifts of ministries through which, by His own power, we serve each other unto salvation.

—*Dogmatic Constitution on the Church* (7)

Christ's redemptive work, while of itself directed toward the salvation of men, involves also the renewal of the whole temporal order. Hence the mission of the Church is not only to bring to men the message and grace of Christ, but also to penetrate and perfect the temporal sphere with the spirit of the gospel. In fulfilling this mission of the Church, the laity, therefore, exercise their apostolate both in the Church and in the world, in both the spiritual and the temporal orders.

—*Decree on the Apostolate of the Laity* (5)

The Church as a whole, including the laity, has a total task which may suitably be summarized under the three captions of witness, ministry, and fellowship. These last three terms are strongly biblical; they appear in the Greek New Testament as *martyrion, diakonia, and koinonia.*

—preface to *Dogmatic Constitution on the Church*

1

We Are All Called and Chosen

This book is about lay ministries, not merely the restricted sense associated with eucharistic ministries, but rather a much wider range of activities merging with the laity's whole apostolate.

A minister is one chosen by God to care for and help others in a spirit of servanthood. No matter how humble it may seem, authentic ministry is a true vocation, a special calling given by the Spirit to a particular person, and recognized as such by him or her.

Vatican II stated,

> From the reception of these charisms or gifts, including those which are less dramatic, there arise for each believer the right and duty to use them in the Church and in the world for the good of mankind and for the up-building of the Church. In so doing, believers need to enjoy the freedom of the Holy Spirit who "breathes where he wills" (Jn 3:8). At the same time, they must act in communion with their brothers in Christ, especially with their pastors (*Laity*, 3).

The laity are summoned to "renew the whole temporal order." This immense task assigned to you and me embraces a very wide range of ministries. Many of these were formerly part of the clergy's servanthood. With the diminishing number of ordained priests and the urgent summons of Vatican II to the laity to be Christ in the midst of the modern world, there has been a basic shift of emphasis.

The revolution in Catholic living in the last 20 years has spread from the deliberate injection of the church into the world initiated by Vatican II. The council's documents explore its implications. Over 2000 bishops at the council almost unanimously passed these documents, endorsing putting them into practice as fully and as expeditiously as possible. Therefore no one can say the documents do not express the mind of the church.

From being more or less a closed society of the chosen, the church in the last 20 years has emerged to participate at first hand in the activities and way of life of people everywhere. It has called itself "the sacrament of salvation for the whole world." Contrary to previous practice, it now seeks to renew not just its own faithful, but the whole of contemporary society.

When the church moves in a basic way like this, it means we lay people have to move too, for we are the church. We are "the People of God" in the world, and a priestly, pilgrim people at that.

Ours has become the era of laity. We are no longer docile, silent, obedient sheep who rely on clerics to tell us what to do and how to go about it, who keep religion piously for Sundays and enjoy ordinary life as pagans for the rest of the week. We have ceased to think of the church as impressive buildings, suitably garbed religious, authoritarian priests, a liturgy in Latin with trimmings of incense and Gregorian chant, a triumphant refuge from the sinful world, the dispenser of first, second and third class tickets for salvation complete with indulgences to give us a leg-up.

We, the laity, are (or should be) now aware that to speak of the church means to talk about ourselves, to recognize the Spirit summoning us to act.

In order to act we must first understand and apply personally the vision of a Christ-centered, people-oriented church that is concerned with all human problems and sufferings. This should lead to accepting the responsibility of ourselves actually being that church with every breath we take and every moment we live. It means a total commitment with no days off.

Our commitment and activity in and for the church entail, first of all, and as an ongoing task, an interior renewal of our own baptismal Christ-life. "The success of the lay apostolate depends upon the laity's living union with Christ" (*Laity*, 4). When we are enlightened and at least partially cleansed by the Spirit, we are able to manifest Christ where we live and where we work, drawing others to him by what we are and by the disinterested love with which we minister to them. Only through the Spirit can we find out what God wants us to do. We need to be in a right relationship with the Spirit and open to the Spirit's direct influence before and when we take action. The faith dimension, the love life of the Trinity, has to be dynamically present in the way we live our own lives or we cannot know what is the right course of action needed for a fruitful ministry in the renewal.

So one of the first things necessary in preparing for lay ministries is a formation program aimed at a deeper spirituality in the local People of God. This program must be aligned with Vatican II teaching and spirituality. *Renew*, *Christ Renews His Parish*, and similar programs promise to provide such formation.

Unless the basis for planning and activity is established in the faith dimension, only a humanitarian force will be at work. This may be good and practically helpful, but it will not be specifically Christian. It will not bear direct witness in the way Vatican II indicated when it said, "A particular form of the individual apostolate, as well as a sign especially suited to our times, is the testimony of a layman's entire life as it develops out of faith, hope, and charity. This form manifests Christ living in those who believe in Him" (*Laity*, 16).

An awareness that each of us, in all our ineptness and un-worthiness, is indeed Christ in action, needs to be the foundation of any lay ministry. He took flesh to establish his kingdom of righteousness, peace and love, and he calls us to be his helpers.

In our times we answer this call by consciously living the role the pope and all the world's bishops assembled at Vatican II have assigned to us. Through our baptism we have been made "sharers in the priestly, prophetic, and kingly functions of Christ" and, because we are in the lay state, we "seek the kingdom of God by engaging in temporal affairs and by ordering them according to the plan of God" (*Church*, 31).

The priesthood of the faithful is a key concept in the shaping of present day theology of the laity. It is closely linked with the church's new vision of itself. This emphasizes that the church is both the People of God and the sacrament of salvation to the whole world. It follows that the laity's main ministry and apostolate is to bestow the sacrament of salvation upon those among whom they live in whatever environment they inhabit.

This is such an awesome vocation that most will simply repudiate it as beyond their powers. Of course it is beyond anyone's powers, but not beyond God's. Having incorporated us into his royal priesthood in baptism, and fostered this initiation through abundant graces, Christ calls us to exercise the powers he has given us wherever we happen to be. None of us is excepted from this call.

Even after 20 years, these and similar ideas are such a shock to many that they automatically close their minds to them. "Me a member of the priesthood? No way! There's a priest up there at the altar. I'm just an ordinary guy. Leave me out of this. I've got to clean the car."

Yet the world's bishops are telling us, "The common priesthood of the faithful and the ministerial and hierarchical priesthood are nonetheless interrelated. Each of them in its own special way is a participation in the one priesthood of Christ" (*Church*, 10).

How has it come about that suddenly (it seems) we are being told such truths about ourselves?

There were long gaps between the Council of Trent in the 16th century, the interrupted, mid-19th-century Vatican I and Vatican II in the 1960s. Trent was anti-Protestant and Vatican I was triumphalist. Vatican II faced outward toward the world with a whole set of new developments and emphases in doctrine aimed at fusing the People of God with the rest of the human race to bless and redeem all.

Trent overreacted to the reformers' identification of the priesthood with the preaching of the gospel, and their denial of a special power given through ordination to offer the sacrifice of the Mass and forgive sins in sacramental confession. The overreaction took the form of emphatic affirmations on sacramental ordination of priests carried out within the church's God-ordained, hierarchical structure. The priest was stressed as cultic, powerful, authoritarian and different. Though Trent did not deny the scriptural priesthood of all the faithful, it ignored it.

Development of this concept had to wait for Vatican II, the council that acknowledged lay people as necessary and gave them a theology of their own. It also altered emphasis with regard to the priest. He was not meant to be a power and status figure, but a servant as Christ himself was. Just as Jesus symbolized his role by washing the disciples' feet—a task normally performed by slaves—so the priest was meant to be a servant of the servants of God. (Holy priests, of course, have always been this.) As another Christ, he was allied not so much with the king of glory as with the Suffering Servant who laid down his life for all of us.

Our own priesthood of the laity is infused at baptism when we are incorporated into the new life of the crucified and risen Lord, who remains a priest for ever. It has to be realized and consciously lived out in daily life if we are to fulfill our lay destiny. Part of the ordained person's special vocation is to lead the community in its priestly tasks and order the various charisms of lay people so that Christ's redemptive work is carried out harmoniously and efficiently. He encourages authentic lay ministries of all kinds. The post-Vatican II priest's main aim is not first to attain his own personal salvation and sanctification as an authoritarian, cultic figure to his obedient flock, but to renew the whole temporal order in conjunction with his co-workers, the laity.

He is not placed "above" them as a figure of mysterious powers and awesome authority to whom all must be subject. Rather, he is "among" them, their "man for others," laboring with them while renewing and sanctifying himself in the process. He has the special responsibility of illuminating their inspiration and vision of Christ by means of the Christ-like qualities he lives out in relation to them, while he remains always alert to recognize to what ministries the Spirit may be calling each of them.

Vatican II's definition of the church as the sacrament of salvation for the whole world widens the scope and mystery of the sacrament, for we, the laity, are the church. Every moment of our lives lived in union with Christ for others is an administration of the sacrament of salvation and an expression of our priesthood. In this way each of us becomes Christ's "instrument for the redemption of all" (*Church*, 9) for "he continually distributes in his body, that is, in the Church, gifts of ministries through which, by his own power, we serve each other unto salvation" (*Church*, 7).

When these oblationary moments are multiplied to fill each 24-hour day, and are also united sacramentally with Christ in the Eucharist, we become filled with the Spirit. In its power we can then both live out and proclaim the good news to all the world—beginning, of course, in our own immediate environment.

We fulfill our prophetic vocation when we bear witness, both silently by the quality of our lives and the purity of our motives, and publicly by giving an account in word and deed of the faith, hope and love within us.

The council tells us bluntly that "the obligation of spreading the faith is imposed on every disciple of Christ, according to his ability" (*Church*, 17).

If we shirk any of our priestly responsibilities, we shall be called to account for it. If we fulfil them like good and faithful servants, the Lord will say to us when we meet him face to face, "Friend, come up higher, for I called you and I chose you, and you answered, 'Lord, here I am. What do you want me to do?' "

2

Koinonia: A Love of Grace and Choice

Lay ministries tend to have as their central motivation one of the forms of Christian witness and servanthood often currently referred to by the Greek names used in the primitive church: *koinonia* (fellowship); *diakonia* (service); *kerygma* (proclamation of the message); *martyrion* (witness, not necessarily of blood).

Ministry in any of these areas should be preceded by *metanoia*, or change of heart, radical conversion and full commitment to interior renewal. Only after *metanoia* can ministries be carried out under the influence of grace and the Spirit's charisms. Only then are they specifically Christian instead of merely humanitarian.

In the following chapters I shall indicate more fully what these terms mean and suggest some lay ministries associated with them. It will become obvious that most ministries contain elements of several or all of them.

The concept of *koinonia*, or fellowship, arises from the doctrine of the communion of saints. Every time we say the apostles' creed, we affirm our belief in it. Our affirmation is based on the experience of Christian community. In and through baptism and Eucharist we are united together spiritually with Christ in one body, of which we are all inseparable parts. We are the Mystical Body of Christ as well as the People of God. We are "family," joined by a vital, supernatural union with Christ and, in him, with one another.

"Saints" means us, the baptized fed by the sacraments, uncanonized, unrecognized members of the Lord's Body and the holy People of God on our way to the wedding feast of the Lamb. United in him, we can no more disown one another than we can disown our own hand or foot. So *koinonia* is the loving fellowship existing and expressing itself within the community of the baptized.

It is not the hearty camaraderie found among the members of a rugby team, or even the more spiritual bond that can exist among a group of people who have banded together in a common life founded upon shared interests and ideals. It is not even the warm love and affinity present in a large, happy family. This is not to denigrate such forms of interpersonal warmth and sharing, but to affirm that *koinonia* is different.

Koinonia shows forth the love bond existing in the Trinity into which we have been sacramentally absorbed. It is fed by joining together in the Eucharist, by faith-sharing, by acknowledging oneness in the Spirit, by participating in reading and praying the scriptures, by seeking, doing and suffering God's will, by ministering to one another in prayer, and through expressing loving kindness for the sake of the Lord.

Since *koinonia* is the love-bond among all the baptized, it includes the dead in purgatory and heaven, as well as the People of God on earth. It also includes the baptized alienated from God and the church. Those who fall by the wayside must be picked up and carried by the others in a Samaritan ministry. A pilgrim people on the move does not discard its dropouts, invalids and and protesters who wave banners, shout slogans and mock derisively from the footpath. All these still belong, even if they maintain they do not. They have been marked by God in the same way as all the rest of us, and they remain his.

Part of the lay ministry of *koinonia* is to seek out and bear lovingly home the lost sheep of the Lord. He is the supreme Shepherd, and we are his apprentices. The ministry of fellowship is meant to be extended to all, especially the poor, the sick, the suffering, the outcast and despised, those deprived of liberty and justice, those in any and every kind of human need—for Christ belongs to, and wills to succor and save, all without exception.

The Christ-awakened heart longs for *koinonia*. Love at the ungraced, human level may be seen and experienced as time-bound, fault-scarred and marred, whereas Jesus' love expressed through believers is known and experienced in faith to be everlasting and holy. In *koinonia* this love flows freely as a foretaste of heaven.

It was about *koinonia* that Jesus spoke and prayed in the discourse at the Last Supper (see John's gospel, chapters 13-17).

> Father, may they be one in us,
> as you are in me and I am in you,
> so that the world may believe it was you who sent me.
> I have given them the glory you gave to me,
> that they may be one as we are one.
> With me in them and you in me,
> may they be so completely one
> that the world will realize that it was you who sent me
> and that I have loved them as much as you loved me
> so that the love with which you loved me may be in
>   them,
> and so that I may be in them
>
> (Jn 17:21-23, 26).

Koinonia is concerned with the commandment to love one's neighbor with a truly disinterested love that has no strings attached. It is a love under divine compulsion to be poured out on others as a ministry to Jesus himself.

"Taking on human nature, He bound the whole human race to himself as a family through a certain supernatural solidarity and established charity as the mark of His disciples, saying, 'By this will all men know that you are my disciples, if you have love one for another' (Jn 13:35)" (*Laity*, 8).

To seek and find Jesus in others is to understand and practice *koinonia*. To gaze lovingly upon him present in them, and to succor his needs, is to be purged of impure motives seeking power, prestige, recognition, gratitude, praise, domination, worldly rewards, emotional fulfillment. This purged love brings to bear against the forces of hatred, jealousy, violence and injustice, those of caring, tolerance, peace, humility and righteousness. Out of them flow actions that cement the *koinonia* to the wider social group, whoever and wherever they may be, consciously relating it to the church's mission to be the sacrament of salvation for all. The Trinity's love becomes incarnate in Jesus redeemed and goes on redeeming us. Issuing from us in brotherly and sisterly love in the Lord, it expresses itself in the joy of self-giving, even to the heroic level of laying down one's life for others in a *martyrion* that need not be bloody.

The contemplative nun, silent and praying in her cell for all those in need, is a vital part of the church's total *koinonia*, as is the humble neighborhood group, its members helping each other and branching out to those in their vicinity, whether of any or no denomination.

Married couples and their families have a special call to witness to Christian fellowship. Their home life is meant to be a cell of Christian witness to Christian love and care so vibrant and sincere that it spills over into the community.

In a priestless (or almost so) parish, *koinonia* is of particular importance. Lacking the full sacramental life of regular reconciliation and daily Eucharist, and possibly having Mass only on one or two Sundays a month, the local church must foster the Christ-life within it carefully. It may need a genuine effort to put aside resistance to paraliturgies and communion services presided over by lay people, but God will reward that effort with special graces. The parish that prays together not only stays together, but extends through the whole community about it the warmly healing aura of its fellowship.

Its members keep the faith in the unfamiliar, priestless situation. Often this will need ingenuity, forbearance, loyalty, determination and refusal to get downhearted and discouraged, as well as sheer effort. Where genuine *koinonia* is consciously practiced by the parish community, grace will be given to overcome human insufficiencies, to plug the gaps with loving tolerance, to have the courage to participate in a positive way oneself, even if shy and diffident at undertaking what has always, till now, been regarded as only the priest's business.

Though circumstances may have deprived a parish of a resident priest, the eternal High Priest, from whom our own priesthood of the faithful derives, is always there in the members of any portion of his body, the church. Jesus is our *koinonia*. He never fails those who remain faithful to his command to love one another as he loves them. How then can we fail one another?

3

Diakonia: The Service of Love

Diakonia is service to others for love of Jesus who said, "Inasmuch as you did it to the least of these, you did it to me." The word indicates a different kind of service from what is given by a slave or for money or for public recognition.

At the Last Supper, when the disciples argued among themselves about who was the most important, Jesus told them, "The greatest among you must behave as if he were the youngest, the leader as if he were the one who serves. For who is greater: the one at table or the one who serves? Yet here am I among you as one who serves" (Lk 22:26-27).

When he had washed the disciples' feet, he explained to them, "You call me Master and Lord, and rightly; so I am. If I, then, the Lord and Master, have washed your feet, you should wash each other's feet. I have given you an example so that you may copy what I have done to you" (Jn 13:13-15).

Diakonia is founded in humility. It springs from a humbled and contrite heart, aware of its sinfulness and dependence upon grace, yet overflowing with love for Jesus and neighbor. This love urgently demands an outlet.

Paul, who in Ephesians has such inspiring things to say about *koinonia*, calls himself "the prisoner of Christ Jesus for the sake of pagans" (Eph 3:1). Anyone who renders *diakonia* to others does it because he is so captivated in love by Jesus that he must try with all his might to obey his commandments and live as Jesus lived, self-sacrificially.

Paul also lists ways in which we may be called upon to serve each other in love through the particular charisms given us. "To some his gift was that they should be apostles; to some, prophets; to some, evangelists; to some, pastors and teachers; so that the saints together make a unity in the work of service, building up the body of Christ" (Eph 4:11-12).

The above are all forms of service that will be obvious. Just as important, and even more so if performed in deep humility, are the humblest acts done in hidden ways to "the little ones" of the Lord.

One danger inherent in any kind of ministry, clerical or lay, is that ambition and hunger for power may lead to "empire building," obvious or subtle. Those with drive, strong personalities and zeal can gather others round them, dominate them and form a faction. The result is disunity, jealousy, infighting, competitiveness, ill-feeling, feuds and numerous sins against charity.

Out of all the words to do with ministry and service that the early church could have used, it chose an everyday one associated with everyday tasks. The word *diakonia* most often referred in common usage to one who waited on table—submissively and unobtrusively.

Those lay ministers who have an innate drive to wield power and influence over others and to make their mark in the community need to quell these urges by remembering the original meaning of the word chosen to designate specifically Christian service.

Jesus spoke of his own *diakonia* when he said, "Anyone who wants to become great among you must be your servant, and anyone who wants to be first among you must be slave to all. For the Son of man himself did not come to be served but to serve, and to give his life as a ransom for many" (Mk 10:43-45).

Earthly honors, recognition, praise and adulation, have nothing whatever to do with Christian service. This ministry is indifferent to them. It cares only for Jesus' words, "Well done, good and faithful servant...Come and join in your master's happiness" (Mt 25:21). Such servants dread only to hear him say, "I tell you solemnly, in so far as you neglected to do this to one of the least of these, you neglected to do it to me" (Mt 25:45).

Jesus reached the supreme fulfillment of his servanthood by shedding his blood, suffering and dying for our redemption. Our own *diakonia*, if deeply united with his, has this redemptive flavor, as we struggle to offer up our whole lives in union with Christ's passion, while putting ourselves at the disposal of others to meet their needs.

In fact, the unmistakable sign that we are involved in *diakonia* is the suffering of deep humiliation humbly accepted and offered up for those we serve. Inseparable from this sign is that of agape love, which is self-giving, personal, grace-full, undemanding, non-possessive, sacrificial, offered for Christ's sake, not our own, asking no return or reward, glowing with the Lord's tenderness, and full of those qualities listed by Paul in his famous panegyric (1 Cor 13:4-7). Humility recognizes that agape love has its source in the Trinity and is a pure grace and gift from God to those who hunger and thirst for it.

It will take a lifetime to attain the fullness of his love. We cannot delay *diakonia* in the meantime, for it is an essential part of our ordinary, daily Christian living. Having to face and accept the humiliation of constantly realizing our actions and attitudes are tainted by a persistent, deep-seated self-will and self-love, is also an essential part of our daily living and examination of conscience.

In the early church *diakonia* was linked with the following: relief work among the afflicted and needy, assisting at the Eucharist, ministry to the unconverted, preaching, personal service to the apostles, prayer, any charismatic gift employed for the community, Paul's mission to the Gentiles, the apostolate and the list of charitable works in Mt 25:31-45.

It is evident that *diakonia* was and is inseparable from the traditional corporal works of mercy: feed the hungry, give drink to the thirsty, clothe the naked, visit prisoners, visit the sick, harbor strangers, bury the dead. And also with the spiritual works of mercy: convert sinners, instruct the ignorant, counsel the doubtful, console the afflicted, bear wrongs patiently, forgive injuries, pray for the living and the dead.

Worth noting is the fact that the servant attitude toward others includes the humility of accepting service for oneself from others. We are all needy in different ways. We all need to be ministered to. To allow another to give us what we need, or what they need to give someone, is to build up *koinonia*. To accept another's love and service can be a very gracious act of humility, filling the giver with joy.

This is what Jesus did when he let the woman of the street kiss his feet and wash them with her tears in Simon's house. She was doing a service (richly symbolic) to him, but he, in accepting, was doing the greater service of showing he valued and opened himself to her love and to herself as a person.

Much of the *diakonia* formerly done by the clergy and religious now devolves on the laity. This is partly the result of the decline in vocations coinciding with Vatican II's summons to the laity to renew the secular order with the Spirit of Christ.

The Council reiterates that this is to be done through service. "Christians cannot yearn for anything more ardently than to serve the men of the modern world ever more generously and effectively" (*Modern World*, 93). The operative word is serve.

Our personal salvation comes as a byproduct of doing just that. The most exalted and at the same time most humiliated and humiliating form of *diakonia* is to live united with the *ebed Yahweh*, the Suffering Servant of Isaiah 52, who was a prototype of Jesus, the Savior and Servant of all, given as a ransom for all. Our Lord likes company in his passion.

This, and other *diakonia* ministries, will be commented on more fully in later chapters. The key thing to remember is this: "The life and death of each of us has its influence on others; if we live we live for the Lord; and if we die, we die for the Lord, so that alive or dead we belong to the Lord" (Rom 14:7-8).

4

Martyrion and *Kerygma:*
Proclaim the Good News
to All the World

Martyrion was first used of the witness to Jesus given by those who had personally known him. They provided first-hand testimony, and it was this, as reported in Acts, that so powerfully promoted in others a belief in the Lord.

After the early church discovered that such witness frequently led to being physically killed, *martyrion* began to mean also the sacrificial shedding of one's own blood in imitation of and witness to the crucified Lord. The saying, "The blood of martyrs is the seed of Christians" reflected what a powerful effect on others this particular form of witness had.

Kerygma (proclamation as by a herald) meant for Christians the public proclamation of the gospel news in obedience to the Lord's command before his ascension.

This good news is not something we are to hug to ourselves as if it were a secret doctrine to be revealed only to the chosen. On the contrary, Jesus gives it to the whole world— "Go forth and proclaim the good news to all creation" (Mk 16:16)—and as we are one with him in his Mystical Body, we are his heralds in our times and in the places where we live and work. We are bound to speak the word aloud, with joy and conviction, for we have been sent into the world at baptism and confirmation to bear witness to the truth.

It follows that we must seriously consider how we are to do this, to whom and when, and whether we are fit to do it. Vatican II warns us, "Since the whole Church is missionary, and the work of evangelization is a basic duty of the People of God, this sacred Synod summons all to a deep interior renewal" (*Missions*, 35).

God desires the whole human race to come to him through Jesus in the Spirit, so preaching the gospel by word, deed and interior renewal is essential to the church's role in the world.

We do not need to be professors of scriptural studies or theology. Four basics are required: (1) a close personal relationship with and faith in Jesus and an openness to his Spirit, (2) a sound basic knowledge of doctrine as it is interpreted since Vatican II, (3) a love, knowledge and personal application in our own lives of the Bible, especially the New Testament, (4) a respect for other people's beliefs and consciences, plus the ability to engage in dialogue, not polemics.

The fact that we are baptized into Christ and belong to the Roman Catholic Church does not give us the right or duty to judge anyone's conscience, or impose our views on them. Here again, humility—an essential aspect of interior renewal—must always be exercised. But it does impose on us an absolute duty to live our Christianity every day and in every way.

> Christ conferred on the apostles and their successors the duty of teaching, sanctifying, and ruling in his name and power, but the laity, too, share in this priestly, prophetic and royal office of Christ. . . . They exercise a genuine apostolate by their activity on behalf of bringing the gospel and holiness to men, and on behalf of penetrating and perfecting the temporal sphere of things through the spirit of the gospel (*Laity*, 2).

Few of us will be assigned the ministry of *martyrion* through blood. Each one of us is called by God to that of *kerygma* in one way or another. "Everywhere on earth [the People of God] must bear witness to Christ and give an answer to those who seek an account of that hope of eternal life which is in them (cf. 1 Pt 3:15)" (*Church*, 10).

5

The Ministry of Witness

How are we to proclaim the good news, to whom and when?

This will depend upon our own level of faith and commitment, the degree and quality of our knowledge and the circumstances and people involved.

The person with deep faith does not seek so much to convince another intellectually, as to convey the joy, fulfillment and wonder of his or her own life in union with Jesus, so that the other can also rejoice in the Lord. It is not a matter of pounding another's mind into subjection through defeat in rational argument. Rather, the believer longs to share the blessing of the good news with others out of love of both them and Jesus.

If we approach witness in this way, we shall be like the converted who, in Acts, are described as testifying fearlessly to the risen Lord because they had experienced his power and joy in their own lives. The more we ourselves are responsive to the Spirit's guidance the more sensitive we shall be to others' degree of openness or suspicion, tailoring our approach and method of proclamation accordingly, under the grace of discernment.

The quality of faith and love we have inevitably shapes us and our lifestyle. This is conveyed in subtle ways to others both by a kind of aura or emanation, and also by convincing though unassuming attributes such as kindness, honesty, lighthearted-ness, guilelessness, strength and courage. We do not need, Pharisee fashion, to point these out to others! Either we have them, or we do not. If present, they are a gift of God and will speak convincingly for themselves through body-language and our general sensitivity to others, their needs and problems, and through our unobtrusive acts of charity.

Hence the council's stress upon "deep interior renewal" as a prerequisite to fruitful lay ministry. Personal faith is catch-ing. It will often do more to spread the good news than any clever talk.

It is essential that ministers of witness have sound knowl-edge as well. How we present that knowledge depends upon both our own intellectual equipment and that of those to whom we are talking. We have to learn to adapt our presenta-tion to the recipient's needs. An overly-intellectual approach puts off the simple and poorly-educated; a too simplified and elementary one will not meet the needs of a lively, well-informed, questioning mind. St. Paul tried to be all things to all people. We too have to try to be adaptable.

As disciples of Jesus in the ministry of witness to him, we must be really familiar with the gospels, if possible the rest of the New Testament, and some of the Hebrew scriptures. Such familiarity is not gained by hearing the readings only at Sun-day Mass. We need to turn often to the scriptures ourselves, prayerfully and personally, meditating over them, asking the Spirit for enlightenment, seeking the words that directly an-swer our own needs and our question, "What is God saying to me in this passage?"

Small-group scripture reading, discussion and prayer is helpful, supportive and often inspiring.

Taking a course in bible studies or catechetics, whether by mail or by attending lectures or seminars, gives a solid, fac-tual knowledge that backs up our more personal one. We should have an orderly understanding of the subject matter of the good news, of scriptural interpretation, and of dogma as it is now presented and formulated. Having a strong faith does not excuse us from the mental effort to acquire an intelligent familiarity with these matters. This is not so we can demonstrate how clever we are, but that we may become better instruments for God to use for spreading the gospel message, as well as answering the questions of those seeking light.

What circumstances and people are we going to be involved with in this *kerygma* ministry?

The answer is simple—any circumstances and any people that come our way in daily life, beginning with those in our dwelling and work places.

An intuitive awareness of what is going on beneath the surface can indicate those circumstances that are suitable for witness, and in which people are, perhaps unconsciously, open to receive it. The same awareness discerns those times that are inauspicious, and where silence and non-approach are indicated. Rushing in regardless can do a lot of harm.

Kerygma begins first in the home and family. Here wisdom and discernment given by the Spirit are also needed. We have to avoid hammering the topic of religion, plus all the "shoulds" and "oughts" and "musts," so persistently and judgmentally that those being hammered are put off it permanently, acquiring such a distaste for it that they never give themselves a chance to encounter Jesus personally. A nonpracticing or unbelieving, critical partner, or indifferent, rebellious children and teenagers, can discourage a committed spouse or parent, who may then react with bitter accusations or heavy-handed authoritarianism.

In such situations, the wordless endurance of the committed Christian can do more than any words to bring the Spirit's positive influence to bear on loved ones. They are not open either to verbal persuasion or witness, but if the believer can be a silent channel for Jesus' love flowing through to all in the home, grace may accomplish the wonder of conversion where human attempts at active persuasion failed.

This is another reason why "deep interior renewal" is essential in the ministry of witness. Only a humble person abandoned to God's will can be a hidden channel of divine grace and love.

At times God, in his own way and time and, it seems, in spite of us and our efforts, will arouse in others the very longing for him that we ourselves thought we were called to bring about. Without God we can do nothing, but even without us he can do anything! Yet grace works in mysterious ways, and many times we are being used by God when we are least aware of it.

In contrast to the divided home is the one where the whole family lives joyfully and intimately together in genuine *koinonia*. The members of such a family, being especially graced, have an obligation to be witnesses to Jesus, to their faith, and to gospel truth and values wherever they go. No blessings are bestowed to be kept to ourselves. They are for generous sharing.

How do we go about witnessing outside the home?

Often it is hard to speak up in the permissive, materialistic, pragmatic environment in which most of us must live and work. It is difficult to find the right way to affirm gospel values without appearing judgmental when those about us, behaving contrary to them, are harming themselves and others. Again, the silent good example given with a love that genuinely accepts the person, but not the deed or attitude or belief, is often the best and only way to witness. This can compel when words would offend or antagonize.

At the same time we have to be ready and well enough informed and astute enough to take any opportunity that presents itself for us to express the Christian viewpoint and teaching on issues that are being discussed and problems of conscience that are brought to our notice. Often this is received with interest and readiness to discuss, if it is proffered in a spirit of simply giving neutral information.

We do not know when or how our apparently casual words will sink in to bear fruit at some later time when grace

produces the favorable moment of true insight—so speak up
we must, whenever a suitable occasion offers.

If we laity are to "penetrate and perfect the temporal
sphere through the spirit of the gospel," we are not in for an
easy time. People may reject our views—and at times even reject us—if they feel we are threatening their way of life. At
such times it is good to remember we are nothing but servants
of God and neighbor. We accept being rejected for Christ's
sake and in union with him in his passion. His sufferings redeemed the world, initiating the good news of salvation. Ours,
uncomplainingly submitted to and offered up with his, will se-
cretly do wonders for the *kerygma*, where our own hasty and
self-exculpating tongues would have accomplished the opposite.

Within the parish itself the laity may now be involved in a
number of activities connected with a more advanced form of
kerygma ministry needing both training and the acquisition of
a formal body of knowledge.

They may preach and explicate the scripture readings at
Sunday Masses and paraliturgies.

They may teach CCD, and give catechetical instruction
to people at all ages and stages, including would-be converts.

They may lecture in adult education of the faith and on
scripture, establish and lead discussion and bible study groups,
address members of other denominations' congregations if re-
quested, study and write to spread the good news, become lay
missionaries, attend theological colleges and take degrees
there. All or any of this may be done in conjunction with their
main ministry of witnessing in the home, work place, sports
field, social and leisure activities, and indeed anywhere and
everywhere that their ordinary lifestyle takes them.

"There are innumerable opportunities open to the laity
for making the gospel known and men holy. The very testimony of their Christian life, and good works done in a supernatural spirit, have the power to draw men to belief and to
God" (*Laity*, 6).

We are all called. Grace will help us respond in our individual ways in the situations in which life places us. Jesus will send his Spirit to be with us and guide us. This does not excuse us from making the effort to become well-informed and accurately up-to-date.

> In addition to spiritual formation, there is needed solid doctrinal instruction in theology, ethics, and philosophy, instruction adjusted to differences of age, status, and natural talents. . . . The laity should not only learn doctrine more carefully, especially those main points which are the subject of controversy, but should also provide the witness of an evangelical life in contrast to all forms of materialism (*Laity*, 29, 31).

One area in which informed witness is necessary is that of ecumenism. The sixth wound of Christ is the disunity and lack of fellowship among the various churches of Christian believers. We can say of this, "Satan looked upon it, saw that it was evil, and gloated."

"Be reconciled to one another," the Spirit calls insistently, whether in the family, the parish, the local community, among nations and among denominations.

Vatican II's *Decree on Ecumenism* is indeed different in tone and matter from the earlier, triumphalist attitude of "I'm always right, and you're usually wrong" confrontation. The *Decree* states, "All those justified by faith through baptism are incorporated into Christ. They therefore have a right to be honored by the title of Christian and are properly regarded as brothers in the Lord by the sons of the Catholic Church" (*Ecumenism*, 3).

It was Pope John XXIII who initiated *koinonia* with the "separated brethren." The Catholic church had not previously aligned itself with the World Council of Churches, nor sought dialogue with Protestants. Its solution for the scandal of disunity was simple—the Protestants were at fault, must admit it, then humbly seek readmission into the one true church.

John, with his wide experience in the East with the Or-
thodox churches, began to change all this. Having announced
that his Council was to be a genuinely ecumenical one, he then
invited observers from churches not in communion with
Rome, seated them in an honored place and instituted a special
Secretariat for Promotion of Christian Unity. John's stamp on
the council was one of dialogue instead of anathema, respect-
ful listening instead of hostile criticism, *koinonia* instead of
emphasis on the "They're not one of us" attitude.

Under his influence the council called for ecumenical
action and "skillful participation in it by all the Catholic faithful" (*Ecumenism*, 4). Catholics were to undergo a change of
heart (*metanoia*), by admitting the church's past mistakes of
harshness and lack of humility. They were to pray, work and
engage in dialogue for fellowship in Christ among all
churches. They were to join in common efforts towards this
with Christians of other denominations, and in social action,
prayer and worship. They were to keep themselves informed
about the doctrines of other denominations and current theology in their own.

They were always to be ready to make the first approaches, refrain from polemics and humbly reassess their own
church's position now and actions in the past.

But all ecumenical *koinonia* and *kerygma* must have as a
foundation our own inner renewal. "This change of heart and
holiness of life, along with public and private prayer for the
unity of Christians, should be regarded as the soul of the whole
ecumenical movement, and can rightly be called 'spiritual ecumenism'" (*Ecumenism*, 8). We have been proud and arrogant,
thinking we had nothing to learn from others. Therefore "for
our sins against unity, in humble prayer we beg pardon of God
and of our separated brethren, just as we forgive those who
trespass against us" (*Ecumenism*, 7).

John Paul II and Archbishop Runcie meeting, embracing
and praying together in Canterbury Cathedral was both the

reality and a deeply moving symbol of ecumenical witness to the baptismal bond uniting all Christians. It was *kerygma* in action.

Protestants have already made great progress in this field among themselves. Various denominations have united for shared worship, and in the matter of doctrine much has been done to reach common agreement. (See the Lima document on Baptism, Eucharist and Ministry, and the ARCIC—Anglican-Roman Catholic International Commission—Final Report of September, 1981). Both of these documents have an excitingly similar flavor to, if not full doctrinal agreement with, the Vatican II ones. Familiarity with their contents would greatly help those Catholics called to a ministry of witness in conjunction with other Christian denominations.

Shared activities of worship, bible study, faith and prayer sharing, and work in the community, and much else, are already taking place and great progress in growing closer has been made. There is opening for a very fruitful and exciting lay ministry in this ecumenical field in every parish, no matter how small.

6

Martha at Work

A variety of ministries may be gathered round the concept of Martha of Bethany, as presented in Luke 10:38-42, and John 11:1-44. *Koinonia, diakonia* and *kerygma* are all involved.

The gospels make plain that Jesus is an intimate friend of the two sisters, Martha and Mary, and their brother, Lazarus. He visits and stays in their home as one of their family. He loves them with the normal range of human emotions, weeping and groaning with grief before the tomb of Lazarus. They, in their turn, love, trust and believe in him.

Martha is a practical woman of action and decision. She is in charge of the task of feeding the guests and serving. Under stress, she is inclined to bossiness: "Lord, do you not care that my sister is leaving me to do the serving all by myself? Please tell her to help me" (Lk 10:40).

Obviously, she is on intimate enough terms with Jesus to rebuke him for not noticing that there is too much for one person to do. In response, Jesus reminds her that material things matter less than spiritual, and she must not become so involved in them, even when they concern works of love, as to forget the spirit.

Though probably hurt at this, Martha's faith is robust enough for her to understand and accept what he means.

When Lazarus falls ill and Jesus is elsewhere, both sisters send him the urgent message, "Lord, the man you love is ill"

(Jn 11:3). There is no need to ask him to come, just as there was no need at Cana for his mother to say anything more than, "They have no wine."

Jesus deliberately delays till he knows Lazarus is dead. He intends to act in a way that will make all involved believe. Important elements of *kerygma* (to the power of God in Jesus, and to the resurrection), as well as *koinonia* (loving answer to the prayer of the sisters and their loving dependence upon him), and *diakonia* (the servanthood of putting at their disposal his power of raising the dead) are evident in the account of what he does.

When Martha hears that Jesus has come, she goes to meet him in characteristically positive, determined action. She also again delivers a veiled rebuke that is at the same time an affirmation of faith.

"If you had been here, my brother would not have died, but I know that, even now, whatever you ask of God, he will grant you" (Jn 11:21-22).

Her tremendous faith believes that, even with her brother in the tomb for four days, Jesus has the power to revive him. Jesus induces her to proclaim openly an even greater faith in the gift of everlasting life to all those who believe, and to the fact that he is "the Christ, the Son of God, the one who was to come into this world" (Jn 11:27).

Even with Lazarus lying dead in the cave, she believes and affirms the great fundamental fact of Christian doctrine, the resurrection from the dead of all who commit themselves in faith to Jesus.

Nevertheless, she remains her practical, down-to-earth self, warning Jesus, when he says, "Take the stone away," that Lazarus' body must have started to decay after four days. But Jesus, after praying, orders Lazarus to "come forth," and the dead man is raised.

Most of those in the world, which means most of the laity, are called to some form of Martha ministry, which is essentially witness, fellowship and service, all founded upon unshakable faith. The ministry, of course, is not confined to women. Men share it, possessing and expressing the same qualities.

A Martha has a deep, personal faith in and love relationship with Jesus. She is practical, active, alert to people's needs, positive in her outlook and happiest when serving others. She can be too outspoken for some, but what she says is usually worth listening to. When she speaks of spiritual things, she has the basics right. She is not put off by offensive tasks, and in a crisis she remains undaunted. There is no shaking her certainty that Jesus can and will help.

The Martha ministry is implicit in much of what is said in following chapters. Just as Martha and Mary were sisters, so Martha's ministry is always closely connected with Mary's more contemplative, interior one. They are two halves of the same whole. Together they cover the corporal and spiritual works of mercy, complementing each other. Together they present to Jesus the problems, sufferings and needs of their neighbor.

In later chapters I shall dwell more fully on Mary's ministry. In the following, I enlarge on Martha's ministry in the form of support, caring and sharing in the parish community. Martha was one of those women who "ministered to Jesus." Such women and men continue to do the same service in today's church.

7

The Caring and Sharing Network

When a porpoise is sick and cannot rise to the surface, another porpoise swims under it to lift it up so it can get its head into the air and breathe.

This is a good analogy for all the various support groups that are needed in the community and could be operative in a parish in a caring and sharing network, drawing directly on the love of the Sacred Heart, the human love of Jesus for us all, the tenderness of the Lord as shown in gospel incidents like the raising of Lazarus. While he went among the people preaching the good news, Jesus also tended their human needs, supporting them with kind words, healing actions, affirmations of their faith, spiritual advice, inspiration, and the warm caring that his whole personality and way of going about things exuded.

The caring and sharing ministry draws also on the loving kindness and tenderness of the Holy Spirit, who is Love itself uniting and eternally flowing between Father and Son. Jesus promised to send us this Spirit, so, in faith in her guidance and love-filled presence, ministers of support go about their work in peaceful, trusting openness to her. They want only to be her instruments to spread *koinonia* and *diakonia* wherever there is need, yet are sensitive never to intrude or impose themselves on those unwilling to receive them.

The following lists suggest some of the ways in which support ministries can operate and so give to those in need the service Christ requires of us. Many others will become apparent to those who are aware of human suffering and long to succor Christ in need in his members. Such people have eyes opened by the Spirit so that they truly "see" the reality of circumstances and needs about them. They respond by saying with joy, "Here I am, Lord. Send me."

In a parish alive with *koinonia* the organized network of caring and sharing people and groups extends to cover everyone. This network is voluntary.

One way of beginning to establish it is by a questionnaire handed out at Sunday Masses and made the subject matter of the sermon, the theme perhaps being the call of Vatican II to the laity to "penetrate and perfect the temporal sphere through the spirit of the gospel" (*Laity*, 2).

Of course, the larger the number of people involved, the less there is for each to do, and though some can and will give a great deal of their time, even an hour a week is a gift the Lord is pleased to accept.

Those with little time might check one of the things listed under

Occasional Home Help:

> cooking a meal
> washing and ironing
> general cleaning
> baking
> carpentering
> fix-it type odd jobs
> lawnmowing
> shopping
> gardening

Occasional Transport:

> to catch a bus, plane or train
> to the hospital, dentist, doctor
> to Mass or confession
> to take elderly or handicapped to shop, craft or social groups, or to visit a hospitalized spouse
> to take children to or from school when mother is sick

Occasional Child Care:

> emergency board of a child for a brief period
> babysit day or evening
> take children for an outing

Then there are the opportunities for those who have more time and love to give—for example

Community Caring:

> be a surrogate mother, father, aunt, uncle or grandparent to children in a bereaved or broken home
> take a needy child on a holiday
> give regular, one-to-one tutoring to a child with reading or spelling problems
> give a home to a pregnant, unmarried girl
> take in or stay with a handicapped child or elderly person while the parents or care-givers have a holiday or time off
> help in craft, leisure or social get-together groups where the lonely, disabled, elderly or bereaved gather to meet and be with others
> help at a crisis center
> do telephone counselling
> join the St. Vincent de Paul society
> read regularly to the blind

have an ongoing, caring relationship with someone most other people consider "beyond the pale," "difficult," "impossible," a "hopeless case"

seek out, befriend and regularly visit the lonely and neglected

Regular, Committed Home, Hospital or other Visiting:

the temporarily or chronically ill, either at home or in an institution, the geriatric hospital or nursing home or retirement village, city or local hospitals, especially to those who have no one to visit them

single parents, especially those who have recently moved to the area or are single fathers

the unemployed and unemployable

new parishioners

long-standing parishioners who have managed to alienate themselves from the church and other parishioners and the clergy

those who have had strokes or suffer from incurable or terminal illnesses, but live in their own homes

paraplegics not hospitalized

pensioners in poor circumstances

widows and widowers, especially the recently bereaved

emotionally and mentally disorientated, problem personalities, perhaps just released from mental hospital

the depressed, especially the suicidally inclined

relatives and spouses of prisoners and the hospitalized children of chaotic marriages

Catholic spouse in a mixed marriage

ex-prisoners

recovering or still-addicted alcoholics and drug users

the separated, divorced or annulled

People who become deeply involved in a type of caring and sharing through which they feel called to give an ever deeper *koinonia*, and where it is obvious they are able to provide valuable *diakonia* help, may go on to receive some more formal training and education to fit them to operate in a specific, skilled sphere. They will be called to this as their special ministry by the Spirit.

Often those who have themselves been through a particular kind of crisis, suffering or failure can best help another enduring the same. Recovering alcoholics work in Alcoholics Anonymous. Those who have found out how to cope with emotional problems can often help similar sufferers. The rape victim or battered wife or husband best understands those in like situations. The hearing-impaired know the difficulties of those like themselves.

Nowadays, the afflicted often band together in loosely- organized or more formal groups for caring and sharing. Many find there the solace and help they need and at the same time are able to support others. Loneliness and the sense of ostracism are eased or banished in fellowship and mutual ministering.

The Spirit is not niggardly in her gifts of ministries. Jesus gives his love abundantly to those wanting to pass it on. If we open ourselves without reserve, God will show us what he wants us to do and help us to do it.

Each parish, once launched on a caring and sharing program, will work out its own priorities, set up whatever central organizing system is needed, and expand according to people's needs, abilities and generosity of self-offering. At the center must be the loving kindness and servanthood of Christ together with the Spirit's guidance, inspiration and bestowal of individual gifts.

As the official Christ-bearer and enabler of the community, the parish priest remains at the core of all this outflow of lay ministries. Through the sacrament of ordination, he has received special spiritual gifts to help him discern how and where the Spirit is leading individual members of his people. It is part of his priestly role "to recognize and promote the specific role which the lay members of Christ's faithful have in the mission of the Church and . . . to ensure that they feel themselves to be members both of the diocese and of the universal Church, and that they take part in and sustain works which promote this community" (*Code of Canon Law*, 1983, Can. 529/2).

He is, in Christ, the heart of his parish. Lay ministries will flourish, and the parish become imbued with *koinonia* to the degree that he himself is the channel of Christ's love and grace and the Spirit's inspiration for his people. The closer he himself is to God, the more open to renewal the parish will be. If he is aware of the full implications of the contemporary church's summons to the laity to renew the temporal order, and wishes to foster all that will enable this to happen, then he will both inspire, effectively guide, and involve his people in a wide variety of lay ministries.

> We have tried to work out practical ways in which all the gifts that our parishioners have may be used for the building up of God's church. The gift may be a very simple and humble one, the gift of being willing to scrub the church floor or weed the church garden. It may be something much more dramatic, an ability to speak, to lead discussions, to proclaim the gospel by word of mouth. But whatever it is, it is a service to the community and the essence of ministry is service . . . There are many other areas in which genuine ministry occurs, often without the people concerned being aware of it . . . It brings a new spiritual dimension to such work, and gives additional inspiration to those who undertake it (*Parish Alive*, Brian O'Sullivan, pp. 16, 34).

The closer and more dynamic the bond between priest and people, the more powerfully the Spirit can work in and through the whole parish family. The parish priest (as long as there is one) is the leader, promoter, facilitator, enabler and charismatic center of the laity's spiritual growth and *diakonia* to one another and their whole community.

In all our caring and sharing, we need to remember that we are not seeking to make ourselves loved and appreciated, but to follow Jesus in discovering and serving the despised, outcast, neglected, difficult, abused, destitute, lonely and abandoned. He showed special compassion to prostitutes, tax-collectors, sinners, lepers, women (regarded as inferior and without rights in Jewish society), the disfigured, the helpless, the afflicted.

He "went about doing good" to those he came across, not seeking out the rich, influential and well-educated, or those whose company would naturally delight and fulfill him.

A minister of caring and sharing follows Jesus. He or she does not pick and choose whom to serve, but simply responds to need wherever and whenever presented with it. This disinterestedness indicates the purity of intention that sanctifies the minister and brings grace to others.

If Jesus is to use us, then we must let him choose how and when and to whom. We act in order to glorify God, not exalt ourselves in pride at our good works and noble charity.

> Each of you has received a special grace, so, like good stewards responsible for all these different graces of God, put yourselves at the service of others. If you are a speaker, speak in words which seem to come from God; if you are a helper, help as though every action was done at God's orders; so that in everything God may receive the glory, through Jesus Christ, since to him alone belong all glory and power forever and ever (1 Pt 4:10-11).

8

Crisis Support

A ministry of crisis support will be primarily concerned with the baptized in the area. Whatever their level of commitment, or lack of it, the baptized of the parish have had the seed of faith implanted in them and Jesus has formally claimed and signed them as his own.

Therefore, the spiritual and specifically Christian dimension is relevant to their lives, even if they no longer "practice" their religion in any formal sense. Ministers of crisis-support are themselves strong in faith, hope and love, or they would not be called to this work. They need to recognize and build on this fact, but with great delicacy, sensitivity and tact. It is of the utmost importance that they never impose religion upon anyone who is unreceptive.

A crisis point in a person's life is often precipitated by a specific, traumatic happening such as the sudden death of a loved one. It may happen, though, when a long accumulation of sufferings, such as intense loneliness, or work stress, or dealing with difficult and/or ill family members, is brought to flash point by some apparently trivial happening.

Suddenly the sufferer knows he or she cannot cope any longer with this situation, this intensity of stress or anguish or demands from others. The overwhelming urge to escape may express itself in actual or attempted suicide, in physical or verbal attack upon the endlessly demanding invalid or handicapped child, in running away, in escape into drugs, alcohol, hysteria or physical collapse. Whatever the cause or the mode of expression, the crisis point is here and help is urgently needed.

Crisis support is unlikely to function well unless there is a crisis center in the parish where people can phone in, remaining anonymous if they wish, or come in person. If at all possible, a contact phone also needs to be open for calls 24 hours a day.

The efficient operation of this center needs to be determined by those involved in the ministry in relation to their numbers, qualifications and availability. Since it is to serve the parish rather than the wider community, its scope is limited and it is unlikely demands will be overwhelming. The important factor is that it is there, and someone is always on call, even only to refer the caller to a qualified person who can deal with the crisis or problem.

A genuine crisis point for the sufferer may not seem so to the crisis minister. We ourselves are not the victim of this particular anguish or stress—the caller is. Our role is to accept his or her reaction as genuine. The problem is of supreme importance and the person in crisis needs our full attention and compassion. This person needs befriending in a positive, non-judgmental, unshockable, supportive but not interfering way. We respond to the need; we do not try to assess what the other's reaction ought or ought not to be.

Often the palpable need is simply for someone to talk to— a sympathetic, receptive, calm, unjudging ear that gives its full attention, makes no demands or accusations, lets the fullness of grief and turmoil express itself, and offers, but never imposes, any further kind of help that seems appropriate and acceptable.

Often underlying the collapse of the ability to cope physically, emotionally, psychologically or spiritually is, in the baptized, another more basic cause. This is the loss or diminution of faith, hope and love in the person's inner self, a loss indepen-

dent of, or only coincidentally triggered by the life circumstances.

The person in a state of despair has temporarily or permanently lost hope. He or she is also unable to believe in and experience God's infinite, merciful love, and to trust and have faith
in a divine solution to his or her anguish and problems.

Christian faith, hope and love are supernatural gifts of
God infused by him and directed toward him. The crisis minister must be firmly grounded in and aware of these virtues, constantly relating to and trusting in God by means of them. He or
she will then be able to transmit some of this certainty to the
one in need, simply by what he or she is and emanates. The
transmission of faith, hope and love is never by imposition. A
suitable opening needs to be watched for, and taken with dis-
cretion and under the Spirit's guidance when it occurs. If the
opening and invitation do not come, the minister never forces
them. God knows best the right time, and will reveal it if we
remain sensitive to his action.

The helper's own virtues are more readily caught than
taught. Sensing the strength of Christ, his gentle, loving acceptance that has no tags, and his experiential conviction that he
and the Father are one as part of the minister's spiritual equipment, the sufferer may begin to long to possess these qualities
himself, spontaneously inviting discussion—but not indoctri-
nation. He or she might say "How is it you can be so patient
with me? . . . You don't despise me, do you? In spite of what
I've told you about myself. . . . You're so gentle and loving.
Like Jesus. . . . When I'm talking to you, and you're listening so
compassionately, well, I feel as if I'm letting it all come out to
God."

Since the encounter is between Christians, prayer is not
out of place, if the sufferer feels that would be a good thing. To
bring Jesus openly into the crisis situation through prayer, is to
appeal to him as the disciples did when the storm threatened to
swamp their boat on the lake. He is always there with us in our
life's boat. The boat seems to have foundered, but if we turn to

and waken the apparently sleeping Lord, he will command the waves to be still and the storm to subside. However, prayer is entered into only with the sufferer's request or consent, or his positive response to such a question as, "Would you like us to pray together now about this matter?"

Because Christ's strength is made perfect in our weakness, the person driven to the point where he or she can no longer cope has a special right to demand that divine strength. Jesus loved the weak and helpless, and goes on doing so whenever, crushed by life, we turn to him and plead for his aid.

Crisis ministers are concerned with both the spiritual and corporal works of mercy. I should like to add to that "the emotional works of mercy." Nowadays, with so much psychological knowledge available, we understand better the powerful influence of emotional factors in our lives.

For example, the person who feels rejected, unloved and unwanted, is wide open to being overwhelmed by a crisis. The negative emotions of despair, depression, resentment, bitterness, humiliation, guilt, and the like can corrode happiness, stability, hope and enjoyment of life.

Because faith, hope and love are such powerful antidotes to negativity, and because within the church we are offered so many ways of receiving and cultivating them, it is essential that a Christian crisis ministry for Christians take advantage of this, but with great tact and sensitivity. This means inviting God into the situation, drawing upon the healing power of Christ, and opening ourselves to the wisdom and sanctifying grace of the Spirit. The minister always prays personally for clients, whether or not the person in crisis invites an open, mutual turning to God and presentation of the problems to him.

This means prayer—from the minister for and together with the sufferer if he or she is receptive, but never forced. It means a praying group for crisis ministers to strengthen one another. It means the establishment of groups of those at risk so they can support one another and pray together.

Groups made up of those with similar problems can do a

great deal to help members. We see this happen in associations like Alcoholics Anonymous, Alanon, rape crisis centers, shelters for battered wives, groups for bereaved parents, groups made up of those with various incurable or terminal illnesses, and the like.

People with similar problems or who have been through similar crises can have a deep understanding of and empathy with one another. They can offer help and solutions that do not occur to outsiders. If led by those who have come through such crises to hope and stability, they can exert a powerful healing influence, especially if permeated by prayer and trust in God.

Crisis support centers need a general referral panel of professional helpers—parish priest, social worker, doctor, psychotherapist, spiritual counsellor, police, lawyer, accountant, budgeting expert, school teacher, nurse. If the parish ministry system is properly organized, a network of caring and sharing systems will already be established to welcome the crisis-sufferer where he or she is most likely to find empathy and backup. Whether the main problem is in marriage, child care, finance, depression, loneliness, bereavement, pregnancy, delinquency, alcoholism, drugs, or some other area, one or several persons or a group will be ready, willing and competent to help and support until balance is regained.

Porpoises move together in schools. Thus they are quickly aware of one in their midst needing support. By analogy, committed Christians in a parish are in a stable condition of outreaching unity and *diakonia*, and so quickly and efficiently react to those in need.

Before God, we are all sinners dependent upon his loving mercy. Not one of us has the right or vocation to judge another. Whatever we do or are, we are all "unprofitable servants."

9

The Lay Ministry of Family Life

Just as the stable family unit is the foundation of all social structure, so it is the church's basic lay ministry. This ministry is to witness (*martyrion*) to the love life of the Trinity (*koinonia*) and their creativity.

All creation has its source in the Creator. The new lives engendered within marriage in the act of physically expressed love flow forth from the Creator himself. That he chooses to use human instruments does not hinder but rather enhances the divine origin of new life. The human parents provide the physical, perishable element, the Creator the spiritual, imperishable, individual core of the new being.

Marriages as God means them to be, bonded for life, partnerships between two-in-one flesh and two-in-one Spirit, bearing witness to the love life of the Trinity, are, I believe, rather rare, at least in their initial stages. Most people marry in relative immaturity. Their lack of experience with life, and at times limited insight into its deeper issues, mean that they seldom know exactly what they are committing themselves to.

However, where their wills are good, their love more for each other than for themselves, and their desire to please God genuine, there is real hope that they will gradually grow into a fuller realization of what is involved. Christian marriage as a

51

vowed, lifelong, sacramental union, gives them time to do
this. The initial commitment also gives them a solid foundation to build on. Of its very nature, marriage is a union parted
only by death. If a couple does not deliberately and openly
agree to this, they have not a marriage, but some other kind of
relationship. Marriage "is rooted in the conjugal covenant of
irrevocable personal consent" (*Modern World*, 48).

The act of love is itself sacramental when it flows from the
mutual longing of each partner to give and receive the utter-
most for the sake of the other. It is then Christed in its beauty,
tenderness, delight and openness to the generation of new life.

> By virtue of this sacrament, as spouses fulfill their con-
> jugal and family obligations, they are penetrated with
> the spirit of Christ. This spirit suffuses their whole lives
> with faith, hope and charity. Thus they increasingly
> advance their own perfection, as well as their mutual
> sanctification, and hence contribute jointly to the glory
> of God (*Modern World*, 48).

Very high-sounding words for the often mundane rou-
tines of married life, with all its down-to-earth obligations, its
petty and not-so-petty disagreements, its see-sawing ups and
downs. But isn't this so for all of us, celibate as well as married?

This is life.

At times in marriage it seems nothing much important is
happening and the whole business is pretty pointless. This, of
course, is where Marriage Renewal courses and weekends give
that upward inspiration that pierces the pile of earthiness and
we once more glimpse that enticing, exquisitely beautiful
ideal.

The ideal is there all the time, of course, like the Blessed
Sacrament in the tabernacle, but it gets covered with a moth-
eaten blanket, a pile of diapers, half a dozen income tax forms
and sundry outstanding accounts. Then we forget the reality
and we omit to honor it either in our hearts or in our daily lives.

A youngish wife recently told me she and her husband always spend the last hour of the day alone together just talking things over, sharing, being totally with each other. An excellent recipe for encountering the spiritual reality and renewing it so it can be lived out in the lay ministry of marriage and family life.

After such sharing, the physical act of love must surely arise from what Pope Paul wrote about in *Humanae Vitae*:

> This love is first of all fully *human*, that is to say, of the senses and of the spirit at the same time. It is not, then, a simple transport of instinct and sentiment, but also, and principally, an act of the free will, intended to endure and to grow by means of the joys and sorrows of daily life, in such a way that husband and wife become one only heart and one only soul, and together attain their human perfection. . . . Whoever truly loves his marriage partner loves not only for what he receives but for the partner's self, rejoicing that he can enrich his partner with the gift of himself.

The church has never been afraid to use erotic imagery to convey symbolically truths about the spiritual union of human beings, either with each other or with God. In marriage the erotic and the spiritual are intermingled in a wonderful way. St. Paul did not hesitate to compare the union of husband and wife with the union of Christ and his church.

As the Bride of Christ, the church is commanded to be fruitful in a spiritual way through each member growing daily in spiritual union with the Lord, and even, when greatly graced, bringing forth spiritual children for the kingdom in the power of the Spirit.

But it must also be fruitful in a bodily sense in that its married members are to bring forth physical children to be baptized and continue the long line of the called and chosen. (I do not imply that only those within the Catholic church are "called and chosen"!)

For from the wedlock of Christians, there comes the
family, in which new citizens of human society are
born. By the grace of the Holy Spirit received in baptism, these are made children of God, thus perpetuat-
ing the People of God through the centuries. The family is, so to speak, the domestic Church (*Church*, 11).

It is the very foundation, speaking humanly, of that
church, for the church is people, not a hierarchical structure
issuing laws, prohibitions and sacraments.

The church is people, people in love with God, who is
Love. The family issues from two persons who fall in love with
one another, and, please God, that also means they fall in love
with Love. If that is so, then their family life will indeed be a
true ministry.

"In such a home, husband and wife find their proper vocation in being witnesses to one another, and to their children,
of faith in Christ and love for him. The Christian family loudly
proclaims both the present virtues of the kingdom of God and
the hope of a blessed life to come" (*Church*, 35).

Though this may sound unduly idealistic, it is perfectly in
keeping with scripture. Jesus set before us uncompromisingly
the duty to strive towards union with God in the kingdom of
heaven—a spiritual, not a temporal ideal. Its chief hallmark is
total love of both God and neighbor.

This is impossible for mere humans, but with the Spirit all
things are possible. Grace supplies our insufficiencies if our
will is good and we let God act in our lives and in our inner
beings. Marriage partners who are also dedicated Christians
can do wonders for each other by mutual encouragement,
good example and gentleness in failure. They can mirror the
forgiveness of God as we are shown it in the parable of the
prodigal son and the tenderness of Jesus in his treatment of the
adulterous woman.

Forgive, forgive—over and over, even to seventy times
seven, and then some more, Jesus tells us.

There's no better soil for cultivating forgiveness than marriage, not forgetting that we constantly and dangerously ask God to forgive us to the exact degree we forgive others.

In a society where marriage is taken lightly by so many, where many are content to live together without any binding commitment, where divorce, single parenthood and abandoned or rejected children abound, Christian marriage partners have a very special ministry to bear witness to the deeply spiritual reality of the sacramental bond of marriage. Many are unaware or cynical of this reality today and need to see it genuinely lived out.

This calls for the humility of acknowledging that, had we not had the advantages God blessed us with, we would probably have gone the same way as so many others, or worse. Maybe we would have lacked the very honesty that causes so many to refuse a church wedding or even a registry office formality (which a friend of mine once likened to "taking out a dog license"!) because they are so disillusioned by what they see around them.

It means facing the fact that, because the church is the sacrament of salvation for the whole world, those bonded in true marriage are meant to make a very special effort to be true to their ideals. They must live them so sincerely and with such unselfish love to their marriage partner, that the cynical will pause and perhaps reflect.

It means living marriage redemptively—facing, accepting and offering up limitations, setbacks, disillusionments, sufferings, hardships, and those sacrifices, small and large, peculiar to a truly Christian marriage. It means demonstrating to our partner true kindness, tolerance, good humor, forgiveness and unselfishness, unobtrusively but convincingly before others, especially our own children.

In such ways we are exercising a most valuable and fruitful ministry simply by living out our state of life in the temporal order as close to Christ as we can get.

And this is exactly what Vatican II told the laity to do.

10

Peace to Families

I am here considering primarily individual and human relationships. They, after all, are what all national and international relationships are founded upon. Jesus reminded us that out of the heart of the good man good actions issued, and out of the heart of the evil man, evil actions. The real peacemakers in the international scene are those who have true peace in their own inner beings.

Often we can do very little to counter the selfishness and injustice at the heart of so much world political unrest and the threat of global nuclear war. We can, however, with the help of grace always change ourselves for the better. Every single human being who attains "the peace of God that passes all understanding" (Phil 4:7) exerts an invisible, powerful, spiritual force upon world events.

If such a person engages in actual peace movements and work for justice, he or she will influence others to see things as the Spirit sees them. This will happen by what the person is rather than by what he or she says or does. The quality of "isness" in a person is his or her prime contribution to peace in the world. It is often so much easier to jump on the latest bandwagon and dash about waving a banner and shouting slogans than it is to sit down quietly with oneself and face a few basic and usually painful questions about how, as an individual, one spreads war and not peace.

What elements in me cause pain and stress to others?

What do I say and do that hurts and angers those I live and work with?

How well do I control my tongue and the spiteful, derogatory or cruelly witty remarks I could, and perhaps do, make?

Am I just in my assessments of people, in what I pay or accept for wages, in what I give to the church and to good causes, in the time I freely allocate to my family and those in need?

Do I really think in an adult, informed way about moral issues like armaments manufacture, or do I take the easy way and chant slogans, repeat truisms, ape others, air my prejudices, parrot what my parents thought, said and did?

Is my attitude: Stop the world—I want to get off; or do I look about me, in awareness of human suffering (especially in my own family and the extended family of the parish), and do whatever I can to ease it, no matter how small my effort seems?

With these ideas in the back of our minds, let us now consider a few specific ministries.

Marriage Guidance Counselling: This is a most important ministry of service to others in the parish. Though there are Marriage Guidance bureaus in cities and most large towns, they may not be specifically Catholic or Christian. For Catholics, the church's teachings on indissolubility, nullity, chastity and birth control must be part of any counselling of marriages under stress, for they are often a major cause of that stress. Consequently, counsellors need to be both trained in specific marriage counselling techniques and also to have sound knowledge of the church's latest teachings on the above points.

As the family is the basis of the People of God on the move, war in the family means harm to the people as a whole. We all know the high incidence of marriage breakup in modern society. The type of counselling that will bring peace into family life and homes is urgently needed.

Those who feel called to the type of ministry that will serve (*diakonia*) and give support and friendship (*koinonia*) to distressed, warring couples, plus clear guidance on the church's ideals and teachings (*martyrion*, *kerygma*) need to be discovered or offer themselves. Their training and expertise are urgently needed in all parishes. The parish as a whole cannot witness to the community outside if many of its homes are war zones instead of sources of the living waters of peace and love.

Counselling Problem Children and Teens: Here also is an area of ministry based on vocation and sound training. War on the home front may be between parents and children rather than spouses, though it is true that the children in a troubled marriage are often forced or influenced to take sides. This sets up basic insecurity, resentment and anger within them which manifests itself in anti-social behavior and a refusal to cooperate.

A problem child is very often a member of a problem family arising from a problem marriage. In any counselling situation it may be wise to consider the family as a whole.

The young in conflict at home and in an anti-authority stance there and elsewhere, are likely to transfer their anger to the church as a parent symbol. They may see God as only an extension of hated parental behavior. They need to be won back, their thinking straightened out, their often violent feelings freely expressed, examined and traced to their origins, their whole selves given the balm of loving acceptance just as they are, with the proviso that with some work on themselves they can become even more worthwhile and lovable persons.

Some people have a natural empathy with the young, with their problems, revolts, sufferings and aspirations. If trained and given the opening, they can perform a most valuable ministry in the parish. The young are abandoning the church in droves. Here is one way of leading them back.

In these counselling ministries the faith dimension enters in as the minister listens with the ears of Jesus.

Group Therapy: A carefully structured, professional system of group therapy has evolved in the community over recent years. Often these groups have a Christian, though seldom specifically Catholic, origin.

All enmity and factions begin in the hearts of people. St Paul's injunction applies to all: "Be friends with one another, and kind, forgiving each other as readily as God forgave you in Christ" (Eph 4:32).

There is no doubt that forms of therapy that lead to deeper self-knowledge, that release inner tensions, irrationalities, resentments and fears, usually lead participants to the attainment of deeper interior peace. This then spreads to others because the individual changes his or her behavior patterns and others change theirs to correspond to a new situation.

A well-trained, spiritually developed, faith-imbued therapist could do wonders in a parish through skillful group therapy. The results would be a lessening of feuding, animosities, back-biting, character assassination and jealousy as the peace of Christ becomes more firmly established in individuals.

Parish members would then more readily meet and mix in order to revitalize their faith, express *koinonia*, pray for one another and the whole world, and initiate programs promoting global peace and justice. This would be the clear aim from the first in such groups, so that a general deepening of spirituality and insight would result, and indeed be part of the therapy process itself.

Through deeper understanding of themselves, parishioners would gain a deeper understanding of others and so enter into a fellowship of loving communication instead of trivial interchange. This, of course, is the ideal, but the whole living out of Christian ministries is a movement toward the ideal of full union with God. Ideals give us both a goal and inspiration. They are to be cherished.

Telephone Counselling and Listening: This is an area where some shut-ins might find a ministry. It would be another valuable means of restoring peace to the deeply troubled and distressed. Here again, training, vocation and a particular

type of personality and voice are essential, plus an even deeper
ability to listen with the ears of Jesus.

These are some of the ways in which the peace of God that
passes all understanding could, through specific ministries,
spread in a parish. Only this peace is the basis for all peace that
lasts and is creative and contagious. From it alone will spring
the right kind of participation in global justice and peace
movements.

11

Open House

Grace builds on nature and perfects it. God takes what is already there, good and bad, and uses it for his own ends. Because he knows all things, he knows of what we are made, he knows we are but dust, and has pity on us. He also wills to bring us to himself, and others along with us, so he wants us to be an influence for good.

The layman's religious program of life should take its special quality from his status as a married man and a family man, or as one who is unmarried or widowed, from his state of health, and from his professional and social activity. He should not cease to develop earnestly the qualities and talents bestowed on him in accord with these conditions of life, and he should make use of the gifts which he has received from the Holy Spirit (*Laity*, 4).

Our lay ministries will probably, though not necessarily, arise from our natural abilities, needs, gifts and inclinations. Some families have a vocation that we might call "the ministry of open house."

Naturally generous, warm-hearted, hospitable, unselfish, and lovers of company, they are led by the Spirit to express *koinonia* through freely receiving into their homes those less fortunate than themselves, treating them like true brothers

61

and sisters, sons and daughters. They are all "family" together.

Though the media is often full of news that is sensational, violent, anti-social and gloomy, every now and then reporters do inspiring and moving write-ups of people who are operating this kind of ministry.

Often these families are in poor circumstances themselves, sometimes they are practicing Christians, sometimes not. But whether or not they are church-goers, they have in their hearts a true love for those in need. Such love can come only from the Spirit. Sometimes these philanthropic people are called "anonymous Christians," living Christ-like lives even though they may not profess Christianity or perhaps any religion.

Those in need may include street kids, unmarried pregnant girls, single mothers, homeless couples and families, released prisoners with no job and nowhere to live, rehabilitating drug addicts or alcoholics, the old and unwanted, those just out of psychiatric hospital and who feel dazed, disoriented and pitifully alone, children who need foster homes, babies with some defect who are awaiting adoption, the shattered partner of a broken marriage, refugees from other lands where they have been persecuted, the physically or mentally handicapped.

Those with the open house ministry somehow get to know when there is a need they can help meet, and they do something positive about it by inviting the person concerned under their own roof. Without being officious or making the afflicted feel inferior, they manage to be actively helpful. Even if their homes are bulging at the seams, there is always a space found somewhere to put a mattress on the floor when there is urgent need.

No matter how late the phone rings, a cheerful, welcoming voice answers it.

Welcome . . . that is the theme of their ministry. Whoever and whatever you are, you're welcome.

The welcome does not always involve extreme cases. It may simply be extended to people down the street and around the neighborhood. Somehow the "open house" people always know who is lonely and needs to be asked in to have a cup of coffee and to meet other neighbors, who has just come home from hospital and has no close relatives to take her in for a convalescence period, who is sick with no one to look after him and could well be put in that spare room for a week or so, who feels old (or young) and unwanted, who is recently bereaved, whose husband has left with another woman, who desperately needs occasional day care for a handicapped child or aged relative.

They find out. Others tell them. They notice for themselves. Their own children report what they themselves have heard or seen.

And they act.

A family that lives such a ministry is pouring out the balm of Christ's love upon others, and the balm of their own love into his wounds. Its members are also being sanctified in the process. The Spirit is overshadowing them with blessings beyond number.

They are witnessing to the gospel message (*kerygma*) and living out the good news of God's saving love for us as they serve others (*diakonia*) for his sake. They are providing for the needy what Vatican II calls a "domestic sanctuary" and Christ is certainly telling them that what they are doing to these his little ones, they are doing to him.

In a very real way their homes are the church in their area. From them and after such compellingly good example, vocations to the *diakonia* of the priesthood and vowed life may well flow.

> The family has received from God its mission to be the first and vital cell of society. It will fulfil this mission if it shows itself to be the domestic sanctuary of the Church through the mutual affection of its members and the common prayer they offer to God, if the whole family is caught up in the liturgical worship of the church, and if it provides active hospitality and promotes justice and other good works for the service of all the brethren in need (*Laity*, 11).

12

Intimate *Koinonia*

To many, the word fellowship conjures up memories of convivial parties, drinking sprees in the bar after a game, rowdy group outings and activities, family gatherings, young wives' coffee mornings, stag parties, pre-Christmas office parties, over-crowded wedding receptions.

There may be elements of fellowship in these get-togethers, but specifically Christian *koinonia* involves the joy, intimacy, peaceful coexistence and loving kindness that are part of Christ loving others through the heart possessed by him. This fellowship has quite a different quality and taste from the boisterous bonhomie of most of the above celebrations.

The contrast is obvious if we mentally compare them with, say, Jesus, Mary, Martha and the risen Lazarus at Bethany for wine, a meal and conversation.

The Bethany family were special friends of Jesus, as were Peter, James and John and Mary Magdalene. Mary of Bethany was bonded to him in a distinctive empathy and intuitive insight into what and who he was, into the quality of his loving and fellowship. He publicly praised her for this, holding her up as an example of someone who was exactly on the right path.

Magdalene loved him with all the passionate intensity of her being and had the courage to stay with him till the end on Calvary and later go by herself to seek his body after the tomb was found empty. He responded to her love with a special tenderness. According to gospel records, he chose to show himself first to her after his resurrection.

Perhaps the most profound and spiritually fruitful fellowship occurs either within a small, closely knit group (a family, prayer group, three or four friends all deeply committed to Christ and to some work for him that they do together), and reaches its peak when it is between two only, the Spirit making an invisible third. The two may be husband and wife, friends of the same sex, celibate friends of the opposite sex, a spiritual director and directee, parent and grown child or any other combination where a bond may be formed in Christ.

Whoever they are, they must be totally and authentically given up to Christ before the fullness of *koinonia* can occur. Then, through them, through their *koinonia*, a very powerful spiritual energy is released for the church, and indeed for the world.

John, "the disciple whom Jesus loved," and Mary Magdalene, both waited beneath the cross, faithful to the end, their hearts consenting to be broken and pierced with his. Their courageous sharing of his agony arose from the intensity and quality of their *koinonia* with him.

And what of the *koinonia* between Jesus and his mother? This was such a powerful bond that Vatican II calls Mary the co-redemptress with him.

> In subordination to Him and along with Him, by the grace of almighty God she served the mystery of redemption . . . cooperating in the work of human salvation through free faith and obedience. . . . This union of the Mother with the Son in the work of salvation was manifested from the time of Christ's virginal conception up to His death (*Church*, 56-57).

Throughout its documents, Vatican II stresses the absolute need for Christians to become united with Christ and become vehicles for his redemptive love if they are to be fully human and live in accord with the divine will. This is the core of renewal. Only in the power of divine will can any of us truly do the Lord's work in fellowship with him, whatever our calling and ministry. "All men are called to this union with Christ, who is the light of the world, from whom we go forth, through whom we live, and toward whom our journey leads us" (*Church*, 3).

Personal relationships that are deeply intimate in the above way are initiated, guided, purified and made apostolic by the Spirit. The Spirit, the very source and heart of *koinonia* since she is the love between the Father and the Son, shapes and directs the human loving energies of those involved.

The Son in one person, for his own mysterious ends, wishes to meet and merge with himself in the other. The quality of *koinonia* established when this merging has been fulfilled has a purity of intention and a limpid spirituality that marks it as especially graced and meant to be used for others. The Spirit, through wisdom, directs this purified fellowship into the redemptive outlets discerned to be the participants' destiny as members of the "universal sacrament of salvation."

Sometimes that destiny may be to found a lay movement or ministry that will have a sanctifying effect upon marriage relationships, or to initiate reform in the field of a social evil, or to devote itself to rescuing society's outcasts and discarded, or to foster vocations to the priesthood.

Sometimes the Spirit's chosen outlet is a hidden work of grace, generated by the sacrificial efforts of the couple or small group to become channels of divine love in a hidden way for others, and conduits for the living waters of the Trinity's fellowship.

In various documents, the council openly acknowledges the role and value of the laity for the spiritual health and holiness of the church as a whole. It holds up Mary as the supreme example of this lay ministry of love, emphasizing the perfect love, intimacy and sharing between her and her Son.

After the resurrection, all those who went out with inspired courage to spread the good news did so in the strength and reality of their personal relationship with Jesus and in the power of the Spirit. Their activity arose out of a one-to-one *koinonia* established for the sake of the wider fellowship of the whole burgeoning church.

When the Spirit unites Christ-lovers for ministry purposes, their relationship shines with the holiness of his presence and direction.

> What the Spirit brings is love, joy, peace, patience, kindness, goodness, trustfulness, gentleness and self-control. There can be no law against things like that, of course. You cannot belong to Christ Jesus unless you crucify all self-indulgent passions and desires. Since the Spirit is our life, let us be directed by the Spirit (Gal 5:22-25).

The concept and practice of fellowship goes as deep as the depths of God, which only the Spirit can reach. Our ability to express it depends upon our openness to grace. To some the Spirit gives a special ministry of intimate, loving communication. Great sacrifices are likely to be demanded of them, and they are unfaithful to their ministry at their peril. The quality of their *koinonia*, however, becomes both an example to others and a source of grace and love for them.

13

The Mary of Bethany Ministry

Martha and Mary have too often been polarized, whereas in truth they represent aspects of the same ministry of loving awareness of and attention to the needs of others. They took different routes to the same end—total love of God and neighbor. One was called to the corporal works of mercy, the other to the spiritual works of mercy.

Because the sisters had different temperaments, they reacted differently to the presence and summons of Jesus. Martha was happiest doing, Mary being. When at last Jesus came after the death of Lazarus, Martha went straight out to meet him. She spoke to him, almost in reproach, but also in sturdy affirmation of faith.

Mary waited behind in the house.

Mary waited—being, not doing.

The time for her to go to the Lord, to act, would be when he himself summoned her. Martha came to her and said. "The Master is here and wants to see you."

This was what Mary had been waiting for—the clear summons, "Come now. I want you now." She obeyed immediately. She "got up quickly and went to him . . . and as soon as she saw him she threw herself at his feet, saying, 'Lord, if you had been here, my brother would not have died'" (Jn 11:29,32-33).

She waited. When the call came, she obeyed, going immediately and quickly. Once in his presence, her first act was one of worship and obeisance, her second an affirmation of faith.

"At the sight of her tears, and those of the Jews who followed her, Jesus said in great distress, with a sigh that came straight from the heart, 'Where have you put him?' They said, 'Lord, come and see.' Jesus wept; and the Jews said, 'See how much he loved him!'" (John 11:33-36).

Mary is at the heart of the tremendous depth of human loving, tenderness, trust, grief, faith and empathy in this story. It seems almost as if Jesus was not moved to restore Lazarus to his sisters and friends, including himself, until Mary had made her act of complete abandonment and remained there both to witness the miracle and to greet her brother.

Jesus went again to Bethany, a week before his passion. Again Martha was busy caring for her guests. Mary did something quite different, and intensely symbolic.

She "brought in a pound of very costly ointment, pure nard, and with it anointed the feet of Jesus, wiping them with her hair; the house was full of the scent of the ointment" (Jn 12:3).

When Judas objected to the extravagant gesture, Jesus again defended Mary, as he had previously when Martha complained that her sister was not helping her.

"Leave her alone. She had to keep this scent for the day of my burial. You have the poor with you always, you will not always have me" (Jn 12:7-8).

There was a deep, largely unspoken understanding between Mary of Bethany and Jesus. She intuitively grasped the mystery of his inner being and his mission. The constant spiritual interflow between them needed few words.

Like Mary, the mother of Jesus, Mary of Bethany "kept all these things in her heart and pondered over them." Out of her cherishing, pondering, waiting, obedience, worship and insight flowed her prayer.

Though Martha was close to Jesus, loved him with all her heart and served him in others, Mary had the temperament and was given the grace to enter into the mysterious depths with him, becoming a direct channel of his love for others. This is one reason why Jesus said she had "chosen the better part." In a way, she had not chosen it, but rather accepted what her own inborn nature indicated as her particular way to the Lord.

The Martha ministry bestows sympathy and help on those afflicted by physical suffering such as cancer, arthritis, blindness, paralysis. Such a ministry is commendable, necessary and what the Lord wants. Most people easily recognize this as a valuable lay ministry.

Mary's silent ministry of withdrawal, hidden prayer, self-oblation, intense communion with Jesus, and perhaps intense interior suffering offers hope to others experiencing interior suffering, especially if the suffering arises from some hidden spiritual, psychological, mental or emotional wound with a cause not obvious to others and incomprehensible to most people.

Mary of Bethany's prayer was contemplative and most contemplatives become members of religious orders whose main vocation is prayer. This way of life has been emphatically confirmed by both recent popes and by Vatican II: "By their prayers, works of penance, and sufferings, contemplative communities have a very great importance in the conversion of souls" (*Missions*, 40).

Though they may be enclosed, so as to create the best possible environment for prayer, they are not cut off from the laity laboring for Christ and his church within the secular order with all its noise, busyness and distractions. Profoundly and spiritually, they "are united with them in the heart of Christ and cooperate with them spiritually. . . . Otherwise those who build this [earthly] city will perhaps have labored in vain" (*Church*, 46).

Here, as elsewhere, Vatican II stresses that without

prayer and a vividly alive interior life, nothing of lasting value can be established for the kingdom by us, the laity, laboring to sanctify the secular order. Not all contemplatives, however, belong to religious orders. Other people living in the world are also called to contemplative prayer, to a hidden Mary of Bethany ministry rather than the obvious and generally recognized Martha one.

Some of these Marys simply follow blindly along a path indicated by the Spirit. They need and love to be alone and quiet with God. This is not self-indulgence. Instead, God makes them increasingly aware of their obligation to pray and offer sacrifices for others, especially for their parish family. In order to respond generously, they deliberately eliminate from their lives much that others cannot live without. For them these things would constitute a culpable distraction from attendance to God's presence, from listening to his voice guiding them deep within their hearts.

These people are quiet, hidden spiritual powerhouses. They do not conceal themselves out of selfishness, for if anyone comes to them in need or asks for help, they readily and lovingly respond. But they always return to absorption in the presence and demands of God, like Mary at the feet of Jesus, opening themselves quietly so he can use them as channels for his grace and living waters. They neither ask nor need to know for whom they are being used. It is enough for them to offer and give themselves, leaving the rest to God.

In every parish there are a few people like this who are either born contemplatives, or at some stage in their lives have been given a contemplative vocation by God. Others become so by necessity, and find their unaccustomed role a most taxing one. These will be dealt with in the next chapter.

A parish should value any Mary of Bethany ministers it has within its boundaries. Though they may seem to be idle, in a spiritual sense they are exceedingly and productively active.

14

A Ministry for Shut-ins and the Afflicted

The local church is a Christed community of fellowship, witness and ministry gathered round the table of the Lord to celebrate the Eucharist. All unite themselves with the offering the priest makes on their behalf. The Eucharistic altar is the center of the parish.

This altar also exists symbolically in the heart of each one who loves the Savior, and has been given insight into his redemptive act and his desire to include our offerings in his. Those who have received this grace of awareness are invited by the Spirit to develop from it a willingness to suffer with Christ, and so fulfill their *diakonia*, the priesthood of the faithful, while administering the sacrament of salvation to others. "Follow Christ by loving as he loved you, giving himself up in our place *as a fragrant offering and a sacrifice to God*" (Eph 5:2).

These people may already have a life of persistent, severe suffering. They may have been precipitated into the mystery of suffering by some searing loss or shock, whose scar will never heal properly in this life. Prolonged, severe grief is a genuine affliction.

Included among the especially invited are those marked from birth by some physical or mental handicap, or who inherit or develop an incurable and often humiliating and debilitating disease. Perhaps the affliction is emotional and psychological, creating personality problems and difficulties in relating to people. Those with some gross bodily disfigurement that makes them feel outcast and unable to mix freely with others and without being, as it were, "on display," are also obviously afflicted.

Others who might be afflicted are the shut-ins, the chronically or terminally ill, the aged and the infirm, those in homes for the elderly, the hospitalized, the blind, the deaf, the neurotic and psychotic whose condition complicates every aspect of their lives, making them painfully aware of being "different" and unable to change.

In one way or another, the truly afflicted are set apart. Loneliness, suffering, deprivation and humiliation are inevitable in their curtailed lives. They have three choices: to give in to misery and self-pity; to rise above their affliction by sheer will-power and stoicism; to learn how to sanctify and offer up all their disabilities and sufferings by uniting them with those of Jesus who suffered and died for all.

> The mission of the Church concerns the salvation of men, which is to be achieved by belief in Christ, and by his grace. Hence the apostolate of the Church and of all her members is primarily designed to manifest Christ's message by words and deeds and to communicate His grace to the world (*Laity*, 6).

The shut-ins and the afflicted are called in a special way to a *diakonia* of communicating grace to their parish, and beyond that to the world. This is an awesome mystery, as is every truth of our Christian faith, if it is pondered.

To communicate God's grace, a person needs to know and to understand what is being passed on, to be motivated by pure love in giving it and to be able to get out of the way so the Spirit can do what he wants through him or her.

Communicators of grace give Christ to others, so they

must cherish the Christ-life and presence within themselves. They need to cultivate the awareness of themselves as being "a house where God lives, in the Spirit" (Eph 2:22). They need to affirm that their enforced, curtailed life situation and their inescapable suffering peculiarly fit them for a ministry that has in it more of Mary than Martha.

Vatican II reminds us that we "can have an impact on all, and contribute to the salvation of the whole world by public worship and prayer as well as by penance and voluntary acceptance of the labors and hardships of life. By such means does the Christian grow in likeness to the suffering Christ" (*Laity*, 16).

Those to whom this ministry especially applies may have few opportunities for "public worship and prayer," but they probably have a multitude for private worship and prayer. Maybe these opportunities are only partially recognized, if at all. Maybe these sufferers spend much of their time fretting, complaining and being miserable because of what they must endure. Maybe they have not the least wish to share Christ's passion and carry his cross with him.

All they want is the good life that others seem to have. They may even be embittered against God for the unfair deal he has given them.

It is a tragedy of lost opportunities, spiritually and creatively speaking, to let oneself be side-tracked in this way from an obviously God-given vocation.

We are all called to be "other Christs," and the afflicted are especially called to share and live out in their own lives, the passion of Jesus. They are invited "to offer spiritual sacrifices through everything they do" (*Laity*, 3) and through all they can't do because of their life situation. They witness to the Redeemer by being co-redeemers with him.

Paul's words have a special application to and for them: "It makes me happy to suffer for you, as I am suffering now, and in my own body to do what I can to make up all that has still to be undergone by Christ for the sake of his body, the

Church. I became the servant of the Church" (Col 1:24-25). And, we might add, a spiritual powerhouse for the parish.

Christ died once for all, but we are included in his redemptive act because we have been baptized into him. He chooses to identify himself, as representative human being, with every single other human being. Therefore he lives out the mysteries of his life in some way through each one of us. We are part of his continuous incarnation, loving and giving, passion, death, resurrection and ascension. All the time he is doing and being these aspects of his human-divine life in us.

We have the choice of willingly uniting ourselves with the way he has chosen to do and be in us, or of repudiating it and saying, "I don't want this way—I want that other way."

Those who accept the inevitable—a congenital deformity, paralysis after an accident, terminal illness, cerebral palsy, the isolation caused by a phobia—can learn how to transmute it into glorious gain through a lay ministry of spiritual self-giving centered on union with the Lord in his redemptive work.

This does not mean relief or cure or even a miracle should not be sought or accepted. What it does mean is making creative what is potentially destructive, and positive what can be cruelly negative.

Suffering has a meaning and purpose. Both derive from Christ and his mission.

The afflicted suffer in one way or another much more than is usual. They also cannot escape from or be cured of their suffering. They need to find out how to use it creatively. "May they all know that in a special way they are united with the suffering Christ for the salvation of the world. The Lord called them blessed in His gospel" (*Church*, 41).

Pope John Paul II, himself a convincing example of how to spiritualize suffering and make it redemptive, has spoken often to comfort and guide the sick and sorrowing. Here are his words to the sick at Czestochowa: "It is through the mystery [of the redemption] that every cross placed on someone's shoulders acquires a dignity that is humanly inconceivable and becomes a sign of salvation for the person who carries it and also for others. 'In my flesh I complete what is lacking in Christ's afflictions.' Wherever you may be, I beg you to make use of the cross that has become part of each of you for salvation."

This "making use of the cross" means that such sufferers' lives are ones of *diakonia* and *martyrion*. They witness to their faith in Christ as Redeemer by willingly accepting a share in his passion. They serve him through their obedience to his summons to take up their cross and follow him. They serve others by agreeing to spiritualize their suffering by offering it with that of Jesus for his redemptive work in the world.

Their work, prayer and ministry is to suffer for and with Jesus in a spirit of servanthood.

"Just as the priesthood of Christ is shared in various ways both by sacred ministers and by the faithful . . . so also the unique mediation of the Redeemer does not exclude but rather gives rise among creatures to a manifold cooperation which is but a sharing in this unique source" (*Church*, 62).

These sharers and servants are living as proxies for others in grave need of grace. They are able to do so both because they have been called and chosen for this ministry and also because the solidarity of humankind in the incarnate Lord is a reality.

Their suffering is "a sign from God that he has given [them] the privilege of not only believing in Christ, but of suffering for him as well" (Phil 1:29).

All charisms are bestowed for the sake of all. Persistent, unavoidable suffering is not imposed as a curse, but offered as a charismatic grace of ministry linked always with the redemptive work of Christ. To see and accept it this way requires faith, hope and love ascending to the heroic level according to the severity and persistence of this affliction and the generosity of the response.

If housebound or hospitalized so that they cannot go to Mass, such ministers of the cross have a special need for the spiritual comfort and guidance of a priest, and to have communion brought them as often as possible. Their homes and sick rooms are ideal venues for house Masses.

Theirs is a representative ministry which, if embraced with love and confidence, leads straight to personal holiness and the sanctification, as well as salvation, of others.

Such proxies are intimately involved in the parish *koinonia*, even though seldom seen by and perhaps unknown to most of the parish. Having made their lives an oblation and their hearts an altar, they are spiritually part of every Mass offered in the parish church.

They are truly ministers of the saving love of Christ.

15

The Ministry of Peacemakers and Reconcilers

None of us can be a peacemaker in a wide sense until we have made peace inwardly with ourselves and others. With others we usually also need to make outward movements towards them, but the first move is always an inward movement within our own wills.

Love is not primarily a feeling but rather a direction of the will, over which we have a choice. We often have little or no choice about how we feel. If our will-directed love is accompanied by warm, pleasant feelings, that is a bonus. Love is ultimately proved by kind, caring actions, not by delicious sensations and emotions.

This chapter is much more about the act of love than the feeling of love. The "act of love" is the beautiful term often used for marital sexual intercourse. If we regard the essentials of this act, we see that it is one of giving and receiving, a mutual interchange, if it is truly an "act of love" and not rape or some other travesty of what it is meant to be.

In this sense it is also a direction of the will. This partner and no other has been chosen. By choice, a lifelong commitment has been made by both of those involved. By choice, they give their bodies to each other. They also give their minds, hearts, souls and entire future.

The will is at the heart of this beautiful exchange of gifts, though much else is also involved.

I use this analogy to illustrate other areas in which "we must love one another or die," as W.H. Auden wrote in September, 1939. In these areas, more often than not, there is no natural attraction at all. There may even be positive aversion, and with reason, if the person has harmed us. Yet in our nuclear age, it is more crucial than ever that we make decisions to love our enemies.

Fulfilling this command of Jesus obviously means a direction of the will, a deliberate choice to will and do good to someone for whom we cannot have any warm feelings at all. Such a conquest of natural revolt cannot be made without grace, and to forgive someone "seventy times seven" as Jesus commanded, is going to need a mountain of grace. But one thing we can always do is to offer up ourselves to the mercy of God. Seeing our humility and pitying us, he gives the grace we crave.

When Jesus prayed one of his most beautiful prayers, "Father, forgive them, for they know not what they do," he was praying for all torturers, betrayers, unjust and cruel dictators, all the selfish, the pharisaical, the seducers of the innocent. What we do to one another we do to him as he writhed, bled and sweated on the cross. Pope John Paul makes this point in his recent encyclical *On Human Suffering*.

When we wrong each other, we do not really know what we are doing. If we truly understood, we would not do it. Only God is omniscient, only he alone can read the human heart. Therefore we are forbidden to judge one another.

But we still do it. We forget we could not have taken the first wavering steps toward our goal of forgiving and being a peacemaker if he himself had not given us the grace to move our flinty hearts and reluctant limbs.

Jesus said, "Blessed are the peacemakers, for they shall be called sons and daughters of God." To be a son or daughter, we have to call God "Abba"—"daddy"—and we have to be a co-heir with Christ as his brother or sister. It is impossible to do and be these things if we deliberately cling to ill will towards anyone at all. Again, it is a matter of the will, not the emotions.

If the parish has a priest, would-be peacemakers are strongly recommended to use the balm of sacramental confession. Their efforts to forgive will be blessed with success, if they are prepared to confess their ineptitude humbly.

What has all this to do with lay ministries?

There are naturally forgiving, tolerant, peaceable, equable, sweet-natured, understanding and almost unfailingly kind people. If they give themselves to the Spirit without reservation, he may well call them to a peacemaker's ministry. Others with different types of personality may also be called, but they will need the rough edges smoothed away first.

Being a peacemaker could mean one of several things:

• Being the one in the neighborhood to whom friends and acquaintances automatically turn in times of hurt and turmoil resulting from cruelty or misjudgment or misunderstanding. Such a person is usually a good listener not anxious to push his or her own point of view. Often the wounded ones are able to see the root of the problem themselves as they verbalize it, perhaps with a good cry in the process. The peacemaker, if Spirit-guided, often knows intuitively which questions to ask, and what advice to give, and will pray with the distressed one.

We must not forget that the wound can also be the inability to forgive oneself, in spite of all efforts, for one's own cruelty to others. Forgiveness, like charity, begins in the home of one's own heart. Those who cannot forgive themselves are not likely to be forgiving towards others.

I often think of St. Therese who, after some years in Carmel, observed herself still falling into a habitual fault. She said to herself with the gentleness of humility and spiritual poverty, "Ah, still at the same place where you began, I see." Then she got up and went on cheerfully, certain that God loved her just as she was, faults included.

• Being in a more deliberately structured counselling situation. For this the peacemaker, even if unusually gifted by nature, most likely will need some training. Because of this he or she will be able to venture more deeply into the underlying causes of the inability to forgive or to accept forgiveness, or the need to keep warring against certain people and against oneself.

Those who operate well in this field have often experienced deep stresses, clashes and situations of enmity in their own lives. Maybe they have had "breakdowns" as a result. Then they have valiantly struggled, and probably been helped professionally, until they learnt how to cope with themselves and their life situations. As a result they have an extra depth of understanding, compassion and ability to help others in like situations. Such people need to be sought out in the parish, asked to offer themselves to be trained and put into operation as their contribution to *koinonia* and *diakonia*.

Their counselling is brought to spiritual fruition when their clients can make a truly humble and honest sacramental confession if a priest is available. Such a confession shows the genuine self-insight the person has attained through counselling.

In all this, the faith dimension needs to be acknowledged and lived out. Too many counsellors are merely humanitarian, and so cannot understand the depths and values of the person who wants to learn to forgive because not to forgive is a sin.

The other possibility for participating in the ministry of peacemaking can include everyone in the parish. If the parish is priestless, opportunities for sacramental confession will be rare. Are we then to carry about our poison in our hearts indefinitely?

Jesus said, "If you are bringing your offering to the altar and there remember that your brother has something against you, leave your offering there before the altar, go and be reconciled with your brother first, and then come back and present your offering" (Mt 5:23-24).

Wars always begin in the hearts of people. How many of us go unthinkingly to communion with enmity in our hearts towards our brothers and sisters in Christ?

Note that it is you yourself whom Jesus said is being accused by your brother. Do you wonder why? Facing up to the truth is not likely to be easy. Maybe a lot of prayer and humility is called for.

James wrote, "Confess your sins to one another, and pray for one another, and this will cure you" (Jas 5:16).

We have to talk it over. We have to say humbly, "I'm sorry I did or said such-and-such to you last week. It was wrong of me and it's on my conscience. I guess I was mad at you because there was a good deal of truth in what you said. Please forgive me, and let's be friends."

Sometimes it's more difficult to do this kind of thing than to fast for a week, but if the grace is prayed for, it will be given. Of course, the results will not necessarily be what we hoped for! There could be "a curse and not a blessing," an angry, "Get off my property, you hypocritical so-and-so!" Or, "Forgive? You've got to be joking!"

Ah, well, we did try. Like St. Therese.

Now we can go to the altar with a clear conscience.

16

Lay Ministries of the Eucharist and the Word

In the Eucharist is the heartbeat of the parish, the church and the whole world. Here Christ is made present among us, comes into us as our food for the pilgrim journey, and unites us with himself so we can carry him to others as part of the church's sacrament of salvation for the whole world.

All of creation homes in on the Eucharist, whether it realizes this or not, for only here is God-With-Us, the one true meaning of human existence, made apparent so we can participate in it.

The incarnate Lord, the Alpha and Omega, is at the center of the whole of humanity throughout earthly time and space. Sacramentally present in the Eucharist, he reaffirms his solidarity with us all, answering our longing cry of, "*Maranatha!* Come, Lord Jesus!"

This true feast of love is where parish *koinonia* can express itself through every aspect of the liturgy, including a variety of lay ministers in action. Here the parish family gathers together in Christ, their priest offering the Mass for and with them as they express their own share in the priesthood of Christ and witness to their oneness in the Spirit.

As all present offer themselves on the paten and in the chalice with Christ for his redemptive work, they witness to the truth he proclaimed and serve others for love of him. The Mass is meant to be the focal point of each parishioner's weekly activities and prayer, and the source of grace and inspiration to live as another Christ in the community in the coming week.

> The liturgy is the summit toward which the activity of the Church is directed; at the same time it is the fountain from which all her power flows. . . . Especially from the Eucharist, as from a fountain, grace is channelled to us; and the sanctification of men [and women] in Christ and the glorification of God, to which all other activities of the Church are directed as toward their goal, are most powerfully achieved (*Liturgy*, 10).

All lay ministers need to have a profound love for the Eucharist and a vital faith that through reception of Christ's body and blood they are given the power to live, love, rejoice and suffer in union with him as they carry out whatever *diakonia* he assigns to them.

Attending daily Mass is itself a most valuable ministry of prayer for the needs of the whole world, and there are those called by the Spirit to concentrate all their self-offering for others in this one act each day.

St. Peter wrote that we are "a chosen race, a royal priesthood, a consecrated nation, a people set apart to sing the praises of God" (1 Pt 2:9), and Vatican II quoted his words and applied them to the laity. All the baptized "are consecrated into a spiritual house and a holy priesthood," are called to offer themselves "as a living sacrifice" as they "exercise that priesthood by receiving the sacraments, by prayer and thanksgiving, by the witness of a holy life, and by self-denial and active charity" (*Church*, 10).

Lay ministries derive from this priesthood of the baptized. Only the ordained minister can consecrate the elements and officially offer them for us to God at the altar. But all of us are meant to join ourselves with that offering in a spirit of total self-giving. All prayer is offering the sacrifice of praise that glorifies God, but the Eucharist is the supreme act of praise. After participating in it "as worshippers whose every deed is holy, the laity consecrate the world itself to God" (*Church*, 34).

Within the unfolding of the Eucharist, the lay minister of the Eucharist performs a duty of loving service that calls for special devotion, reverence, dedication and humility. No human being is worthy to consecrate, receive or give the Lord's body to others. Yet he calls some to do this, and they respond in awe and overwhelming love if they realize the significance of their calling.

If they have been chosen for the right reasons, and not because they have influence, social position, connections with the hierarchy, or have lived in the parish all their lives, and if they have been properly instructed and prepared before induction, then they will come to their ministry with deep humility.

Their devotion to the Eucharist will be evident in the sacrifices they make to attend Mass and receive communion on at least some weekdays as well as Sundays. When giving communion to others, they also make a spiritual, silent impact through the quality and intensity of their own faith, hope and love.

All lay ministries, if faithfully carried out, lead to growth in holiness in both the minister and those they serve. But of its very nature the eucharistic ministry offers special graces if the minister is prepared to receive them. It costs to open oneself to receive a grace, and from those to whom much is given a great deal is going to be asked by God. Our individual response to his proffered graces is a matter of our own choice, and our willingness to accept the consequences flowing from those graces.

Every time ministers of the Eucharist hold the Lord between their fingers, Jesus asks them to make a deeper commitment of themselves to him and others. He asks that their hearts be opened completely to become one with his heart, that they submit to his usage in whatever way he desires, entering into a total sharing of his servanthood with him.

Only those who live each hour of each day in unremitting effort to respond to this summons to total commitment, know what the cost is. They are the ones who are responding fully to the vocation of eucharistic minister.

As well as distributing communion at parish Masses, the minister may be appointed to take the Eucharist to the sick or housebound or elderly. This is a special extension of his ministry, involving personal relationships with people who may be in need of spiritual comfort and refreshment, conversation as well as sacrament.

Often such people are lonely and need befriending. They need someone to talk to, to share suffering or problems with, to cheer them up, to give *koinonia*. The minister's personal warmth and empathy are part of the eucharistic presence of Jesus that he or she bears sacramentally. Eucharistic ministers come to give Jesus in all possible ways to the people they serve.

A minister of the Eucharist may also be called upon to baptize, to perform the rite of viaticum for those seriously ill or in danger of death, to lead and conduct paraliturgies and celebrations of the Word or to read the gospel.

In areas of priest shortages or religious persecution, the minister's role becomes extremely important, and his or her duties diverse. As priests die and there are no newly ordained ones to take their place, a body of reliable, spiritually awakened, competent, dedicated, reverent and freely available eucharistic ministers in a parish becomes a necessity.

Another vital liturgical minstry is that of ministers of the word. Proclaiming the first reading, the psalm response, the second reading, and prayers of the faithful at the Sunday eucharistic liturgy is not a ministry to be lightly undertaken.

What are the qualities called for?

The reader needs a personal knowledge and love of the Bible. To proclaim the reading selected for the liturgy with all the nuances of meaning in a passage of scripture, he or she should be able to relate that passage to the rest of the Bible and to have the kind of spiritual enlightenment that comes only from prayerful study and personal application of God's word to the reader's own life.

Correct pronunciation of the names of people and places, and of any other unfamiliar words is essential. I once heard a reader tell us about an urchin instead of a eunuch throughout the whole of the passage about Philip and the Ethiopian.

The reader's delivery must be first class: clear voice and diction, pitched to be heard by everyone in the church, taking into account the presence or absence of a microphone, its qualities and correct placement.

The reader needs good eye contact, looking at the people frequently without losing his or her place. The delivery should be unhurried, the tone of voice and modulations in keeping with the type of passage. The reader's own sincerity and faith should be evident in every word. This of course implies conscientious practice beforehand.

The reader proclaims God's word in a ministry of *kerygma*, and so must aim at getting through to everyone present, having beforehand asked the help of the Holy Spirit. The reader's aim is the glory of God, not his or her own self-importance.

Reverence and dignity should be apparent as the reader approaches and leaves the sanctuary and stands at the ambo. If leading the congregation in the psalm and prayers of the faithful, the reader's manner should make it apparent that this is an act of worship done together.

A really good reader—spiritually as well as technically — is a great asset to the Mass. His or her expertise can well be used in expanding the ministry to include training others to proclaim the Word of God in a similar way, though with each individual's personal stamp of style and authenticity.

17

Ministers of Hospitality

It is unfortunately true that people repeatedly say they are not made welcome at the Catholic church, that other people do not bother to greet or stop to talk to them, and that no one finds out whether they are new parishioners, transitory visitors, regular vacationers, or members of the parish that no one has taken notice of for years.

One young mother said desperately to me, "I've finally thrown in my lot with the Baptists. I've got to have that fellowship, and they give it. You don't get it in our church."

Another, the Anglican wife of a non-practicing Catholic who wanted his four children brought up as Catholics but did nothing about it himself, did a religion course herself, took them to CCD, had them baptized, and then the marriage broke up. With custody of the children, she moved to another town. Here she put them in the Catholic school and took them to Mass herself every Sunday.

No one called at her home, welcomed her to the parish, invited her to join anything, spoke to her after Mass, made an effort to include her or draw her into the church. With different treatment she would probably have become a Catholic. She was lonely as a single parent with a traumatic background in a strange place where she knew no one and her children were of a different denomination from herself.

Such stories could be added to indefinitely, covering all age groups and circumstances.

As parishes become more and more lay-oriented and organized with a variety of ministries, loneliness will become much less of a common problem in our church.

The Sunday eucharistic liturgy is the usual occasion for parish members to gather. Below are listed several ministries that, if put into operation, could help make people feel at home.

Welcomers are people who relate easily to others, strangers as well as friends, who have warm manner and smile, a friendly tone of voice and a good memory for faces and names. These people have the loving kindness of Jesus in their hearts.

Their ministry is to be at all entrances and exits before and after Sunday Masses, wearing clearly visible nametags, greeting people, introducing themselves, giving information verbally and by printed bulletins on activities going on in the parish, welcoming new parishioners and visitors with maybe the presentation of a little buttonhole posy and an invitation to the parish coffee in the hall after Mass.

Both women and men should be welcomers. Enough should be scheduled for each Mass every Sunday to be available to as many people as possible. They should mingle with people outside after Mass, noticing especially those on their own, or looking lonely or lost, or inclined to slip away as if they are feeling they do not fit in and no one is going to bother to speak to them.

The ministers' aim is to help such people feel they belong, without pressuring or being overwhelming or garrulous. If they will come for a cup of coffee in the hall, then introductions can more readily be made there. Having found out the interests of the lonely parishioners or newcomers, the welcomers can introduce them to the leaders of various groups, or arrange for those leaders to phone them.

In a *koinonia* parish no one should feel left out. Some people are much less gregarious than others and prefer to be alone a lot of the time. That is no excuse for their not being made welcome and told where and how they can meet up with others if they wish to do so.

Ushers are also ministers of hospitality in their unobtrusive way. If they smile and are gracious as they show people to their seats, that is in itself an act of kindness and welcome.

Newsletter distributors not only stand at the entrances making sure everyone receives a sheet, but by their smiles and warm manner also help diffuse the spirit of loving kindness.

Although the *musicians* for the liturgy—instrumentalists, choir or congregation singers—are not officially ministers of hospitality, their ministry of making a glad and beautiful sound has a great deal to do with helping people experience the Eucharist as a joyful occasion. Those who have been feeling lonely and left out can scarcely remain so when everyone is singing and expecting them to join in.

It may seem odd to speak of a ministry at the *Sign of Peace*, yet are we not ministering peace, love and friendship to one another as we exchange this liturgical greeting? We are certainly meant to be! Do we smile warmly? Do we say the person's name if we know it? Are we afraid to hug someone who looks forlorn and alone? Do we give a real handclasp, or only a limp, cold-fish one? Do we turn reluctantly and austerely while we merely nod to one person alongside, or do we make a point of cheerfully and warmly greeting the half dozen nearest us? Do we include the children?

If, after Mass, we see the people we have exchanged a sign of peace with, do we smile at them and look as if we are glad to encounter them again?

If everyone entered into a Sign of Peace ministry, the whole congregation would feel both welcoming and welcomed.

Liturgy for the Children is really a *kerygma* ministry, but it does much to make the children feel welcome and valued participators in the parish family Eucharist. Father Brian O'Sullivan in his inspiring little book *Parish Alive* details how the children and young people are ministered to liturgically in his parish.

The Sunday liturgy arranged for the different age groups is closely related to the youth groups for the same ages, so that the children already know one another. Even the pre-schoolers are part of a club for young mothers of under-fives, and some of these mothers help in their Sunday activities.

A special liturgy of the word is devised for the children and takes place between the initial greeting and penitential rite and the end of the homily. During this time, having processed from the church with their own bible and candles, they gather in age groups in the hall for activities and scripture study based on the day's readings.

A mixture of trained teachers and parent helpers supervise. Songs are taught and sung, and there is a procession back into the church at the offertory.

This kind of arrangement involves parents deeply, as well as making all age groups of the young feel welcome, wanted, and a living part of the liturgy that they have been helped and taught to understand.

The weekly bulletin and monthly or quarterly parish magazines are an important means of communication. They are also part of the welcoming ministry because they make newcomers and others conversant with what is available in the parish for spreading *koinonia.*

—They give practical information such as telephone contact numbers, dates and places where groups meet.

—They list what has happened in the last week or month, one hopes chattily and with a touch of humor. They advertise what is coming up in the future, one hopes in an inviting, interesting manner.

—They give the parish priest an opportunity for a personal message to his parishioners in a more permanent form than the Sunday homily or the exchanges outside the church after Mass.

The editorship of the parish magazine is a lay ministry in itself and a means of keeping a finger on the parish pulse. To spread the news is to make contact with people, and contact helps to make parishioners feel welcome, wanted, belonging and at home.

The foregoing are only a few suggestions regarding a Ministry of Hospitality. Any experienced priest or active parishioner or lonely newcomer could probably add to them. Different parishes have different needs according to their predominant makeup. People need to get together, decide what their parish's needs are in this area, and work out the best ways to meet those needs.

18

Extended Ministry

In this book I have written mostly about lay ministries within the parish membership and structure. This is not because of a failure to recognize the importance of their function beyond parish confines. On the contrary. It is precisely to fit people to perform ministries imbued with the Spirit's guidance and love in the wider social milieu that they need to be nurtured first in the extended family *koinonia* and *diakonia* of the parish.

Vatican II's *Pastoral Constitution on the Church in the Modern World*, together with papal encyclicals preceding and following it, clearly show that the church has emerged from protective barriers erected at the time of the Reformation into an openness to the modern world and a deep, wide pastoral concern for all peoples everywhere.

Issues of social justice, political freedom, poverty and nuclear threat, are in the forefront of her awareness. She expects, and even commands us to "go forth into the whole world" with an enlightened Christian conscience, and live there as disciples sensitive to all kinds of human suffering and exploitation who do all in their power to ease that suffering and right those social wrongs.

We are to have such reverence and care for others as to regard every person as our neighbor, as having a right to our *diakonia*.

The council lists as among the "infamies" we must work to eliminate:

> any type of murder, genocide, abortion, euthanasia, or willful self-destruction; whatever violates the integrity of the human person, such as mutilation, torments inflicted on body or mind, attempts to coerce the will itself; whatever insults human dignity, such as subhuman living conditions, arbitrary imprisonment, deportation, slavery, prostitution, the selling of women and children, as well as disgraceful working conditions, where men are treated as mere tools for profit, rather than as free and responsible persons . . . (*Modern World*, 27).

It examines human solidarity, imbalances and changes in contemporary society, responsibility and participation, the sanctity of marriage and the family, recognizing and implementing the right to culture, labor and leisure, ownership and property, political participation, the fostering of peace, the arms race, international organizations, dialogue where there are differing convictions and many other contemporary issues.

The whole tenor of the document is that we, Christ-bearers by baptism, are meant to be out there in the forefront of the battle against evil in all its forms. It is our duty to participate, to be fully informed, to weigh issues wisely and calmly, to concentrate our attention on the human beings that are deprived and suffering, and to act.

> This Council exhorts Christians, as citizens of two cities, to strive to discharge their earthly duties conscientiously and in response to the gospel spirit. They are mistaken who, knowing that we have here no abiding city but seek one which is to come, think that they may therefore shirk their earthly responsibilities. For they are forgetting that by the faith itself they are more than ever obliged to measure up to these duties, each according to his proper vocation (*Modern World*, 43).

There is to be no split between our faith and our daily lives. Religion is not to be kept for Sunday and church rituals, but is to be applied constantly and in all kinds of ways right where we live, work and relax. St Paul told us to do whatever we do to the glory of God, and to pray all the time. This is possible only if our faith and daily living are so enmeshed that we cannot tell one from the other.

The council urges us to use our lay initiative and lay knowledge of the intricacies, ills, strengths and social ties and obligations of our environment. Our role is to live and work there, involved in its issues and personal relationships, responding to these according to our individual gifts and vocation.

The result, as pointed out already in previous chapters, is that we lay people undertake the responsibility of bringing the Spirit's influence to bear upon the events of our daily lives and the people we encounter there. This is to be done by example, dialogue, acts of charity, and faithfulness to the Christ within ourselves and others, rather than by condemnations, anathemas, heated arguments and acts of violence.

It is to be done by living out and applying gospel values, so we must have studied and absorbed those gospels.

We can see that in the list already cited (and this touches only a small example from the total areas open to lay action) there are many opportunities for our ministry. These may be individual or group ministries, those requiring extensive training and those requiring little, those to be applied in one's immediate environment and a few calling one to other lands and alien cultures.

We are the church, and we must reach out.

My vision of *koinonia, diakonia* and *martyrion* begins in the local parish, with Christ sacramentally present at its center, his life spreading out through all the baptized gathered round their church's altar to break bread together, share the love feast, and be spiritually fed by it. Then it pours itself out prodigally, exactly as do the sun's rays of light and warmth, to encompass all our environment, our nation, and the world community beyond.

The aim is that Christ may be all in all.